Out on a Limb...

By

V.A. Buck

ISBN: 1-4140-0224-6 (e-book)
ISBN: 1-4140-0225-4 (Paperback)
ISBN: 1-4140-0226-2 (Dust Jacket)

This book is printed on acid-free paper.

1stBooks – rev. 11/26/03

Acknowledgments

To my sister, for giving me so much love, support and encouragement while writing this novel. She anxiously awaited each chapter by email, critiquing each one and giving me a two-thumbs-up. I couldn't have done this without you Bubba!

To my parents: I never knew my letters to you over the years were proof enough for you that I could do this. I will be forever grateful.

To all of my wonderful friends: Thank you for inviting me to come out and play for awhile. The endless summer days spent golfing, fishing and cooking out were my saving grace from insanity.

To Sabrina: Your patience with me, while writing this, is a huge devotion.

Prologue

I remember the day I left. It was a cold, crisp March morning and as we stood by the moving van trying to decide who was going to take the cat, I knew in my heart that this was it and I would never see her again. I would never feel her arms around me, holding me like she never wanted to let go.

Once you have spent ten years with someone you dearly love, just to walk away and forget the memories was hard. Driving those nine and half-hours to Tennessee was one of the hardest things I have ever had to do. I knew as I crossed over the Ohio border into Kentucky, I would never return. Leaving everyone I knew and loved, and not knowing what was about to come was the literal "fear of the unknown".

I remember how hard I cried when I finally realized it was over. All I could envision was her face and the tears streaming. The house would be empty of all my things. The garden, bare. No more flowers to plant or yard to mow. No more shoveling snow off the driveway. No more trips to Cleveland to see her family. I knew I would lose that closeness with her mom. I would lose more than I ever thought. Photo albums could not replace those moments nor would there be any more pictures to take. I'm not sure my heart or I could bear this. She had been my entire family.

I barely remember driving from city to city, stopping at each one along the way for gas and a Pepsi. It was the caffeine I needed to stay awake. Tuning into each local radio station and hearing love songs made me cry even harder. But I needed the noise of the radio's sound to keep me going. I had to make it home before dark and I was already exhausted. I knew I had to do this. I had to go home and face whatever it was that kept me from coming home to begin with.

My journey home became only the first obstacle I had to overcome. I'm not even sure how many "obstacles" I had to endure, but I knew there would be many. I guess the first obstacle was coming home to where we first began and facing that cold reality. For the first time in ten years, I was truly alone. No one to hold. No one to share my day or go out to eat with. No one to love. The pain I felt was immeasurable. I have never known that kind of pain. It was as if I was grieving over a death. Maybe my soul died that day and I was grieving over my own. I wasn't sure. I Just knew I was dead inside. But now, I had to find a way to survive without her. I wasn't ready to meet or be around anyone. I just wanted to be alone. I knew I was depressed, but I didn't care. I was living in a cabin in the woods and had all I needed. A fireplace to keep me warm and my cats to keep me company. I just needed to survive five minutes at a time. I felt no one could ever imagine what I was going through.

Keeping a journal kept my thoughts and analogies in perspective. Saying out loud what I felt was one thing, but actually putting it down on paper was like speaking the "truth". The old saying that 'the truth will set you free' is actually true. It hurts like hell, but it's true.

The truth was that I had never felt more alone in my life. I didn't know who I was anymore. I had lost my individuality and all faith in myself. I wondered if I would ever be able to give my soul again. Technically, she still had my soul. Our celebration of love had always given me strength. Our inseparability, I thought was forever. Our security was liberated from within. She made me feel everything. Where had all that gone? What I needed now was to actually make my own decisions. "It's all about the healing process and moving on with my life", my therapist would say. I just needed to take some kind of a direction. A healing direction.

Chapter 1

The thought of having a child was something that had remained in my mind for some time. We had always talked about having a child together, but it never developed. It seemed it's all I thought about. I wanted a son and to give him my birth name. I wanted a family of my own. This would be my unconditional love. Perhaps this was the *healing* direction I needed to pursue. It was my own direction and only I knew what I needed. But, so did my heart. My reflection of passion would be my own celebration of love. This would be my new life.

I feared to dream the passion because I didn't want another failure to face. I just wanted to overcome the fantasy of finding that perfect person I would spend the rest of life with, because there wouldn't be another partner. There wouldn't be whispers of love and passion or a sense of peace. This person just doesn't exist and never will. The only love in my life would be the first touch of my inner soul to my newborn son. All the nostalgia of a family could make it happen. I had to make it happen. I knew I would be a good parent. My inner nature of intimacy was to nurture an innocent and trusting soul. No one could do it better. I had to take one last look in the mirror to see what was about to change forever. This would be a love for life.

This journey to celebrate love was a promise to myself to live a simple life. That's all I've ever wanted was a simple life. To be awakened by rain on a tin roof, or to hear a kitten's first meow. Building a fire in the fireplace on a bitter and snowy, winter's night. Watching daffodils bloom in the spring. What could move my soul more than the changing of winter into spring? The beginning's of a new life emerging from a long slumber. A stream's resilience of being frozen and confined had suddenly developed into a natural fountain of flowing ice and water. What an amazing feat!

The simplest of things had been forgotten and overlooked. My soul had been dead too long. How could I have forgotten all these simple things that made me happy? Where was my devotion to myself? Where was my sense of peace? My freedom to explore and love life had been frozen in time. I had to make the change in my heart and soul to live again. I had to risk the future of my sanity and loneliness or this journey would quickly end only to be another failure. I didn't want that. I had to find resolve in my heart that this was the ultimate sense of peace.

Surprisingly, this was the moment I realized I needed to commit. Commit to a life-changing decision that would not only change me forever, but also effect my relationship with my friends and family. I wondered what they would think of my decision. It didn't matter. Of course it mattered, but that wasn't going to make me change my mind if they didn't approve. This was who I had become. I was strengthened by this overwhelming desire to live life. I had found the inner peace. I felt God was smiling down on me. Perhaps I had finally found my purpose in life.

I had struggled for so long, trying to find the answer of what I was supposed to do in this world. I could do almost anything, but I had no *passion*. I didn't have that drive to wake up in the morning as if I couldn't wait to get 'there', wherever 'there' was. I didn't like what I was doing. I felt trapped and unappreciated. I knew I had more to offer, but I couldn't offer any more because of my insecurity in failing. Right now, I just needed to feel some comfort. The only comfort I could think of was music. The gentle and comforting sounds of Handel, Bach, and Haydn. I found each sonata took me to a higher level of thought and sensitivity. They say that music stirs the soul and soothes the savage beast. It was as if every chord of an orchestra heightened my senses. An Instrument of spirits, as if an orchestrated recital of emotion overtook me. I felt myself swaying to the movement of each piece as if it had been eloquently performed just for me. It took me to a different level of comfort. I felt liberated and swept away by the immense but restful, compositions. Each stroke of the piano's keys was like each facet of my life unfolding in a much clearer light. It was the only way to escape for at least enough time to grasp a full breath and relax my entire body, mind and soul. It was as if a huge load had been lifted because of the choices I made.

My simple choice to pursue having a child made me feel alive. I wondered why had this choice been such a struggle to conquer and how could I have lost so much of my individuality? It seemed so clear to me now. All I could do now was move forward one day at a time. I found I had so much to look forward to, except telling my parents.

V.A. Buck

Chapter 2

Finding the strength to tell my parents was like finding the courage to admit you have cancer. I knew they would be hard to face and they would never understand or approve of my decision to have a child. In their eyes, I wasn't the typical mother-to-be type. Having this child without a father or even being unmarried would be my father's argument.

My father, the Southern Baptist Deacon, would argue that it was more or less a sin to bring a child into this world unmarried and raising it on my own would be devastating to the child. He is of the Old World. He believes that a woman should be in the kitchen cooking for him, doing his laundry, and saving every penny he makes. He can spend his money on what he thinks would be a good investment. He's a financial wizard, but never tells you how to invest or clues you in on any secrets for fear you might catch on to him and find out how he actually ticks.

Mother, on the other hand, is also the typical mother. She is of the Old World, too and believes you should be a virgin when you marry. She would argue that this would hurt the child more than anything. She wouldn't think it would be fair to the child. She says that a child needs a father and a mother figure for the child to be well balanced. She believes that a woman should be strong and not accept the senseless games from men. I think she believes that men are weak and need reaffirmation that they are loved. She is constantly analyzing about such things. She is very smart and could have been a doctor or teacher in her day, but I think she gave up many career possibilities to become a mother and a wife. He came first in all things. Because of that, I believe she lost herself along the way.

That's the way it was back then. You did for your husband and your children. You gave up yourself for your family. Now, I have everything I could want, even my career. All I need now is to share my life with my child. Explaining all this to them will be like trying to ride a bicycle in the ocean. It won't make any sense, it will be too difficult, and I'll get hurt trying. I can imagine this conversation already. They wanted to be grandparents, but not like this. He will say it's the wrong approach. She will say it's too hard for a single mother to raise a child. They will say all the negatives to try and keep me from having a baby. They might even say that I'm not cut out to be a mother.

Honestly, it won't matter what they say. If they want to be a part of their grandchild growing up, they can. It will be up to them. All I know is that having this conversation with them will be uncomfortable because I will be trying to defy the odds. It's not the 1950's. It is the time when women are more able, willing, feminine, and defiant about everything. It is the time when women have to prove themselves not only to the world, but also to themselves that they are capable of accomplishing anything. We don't need a man for anything. Well, except for one thing in my case, making a baby. That's one thing time will never change.

~

As I flipped through the phone book yellow pages, I caught myself looking for the words "sperm bank." Embarrassed, I laughed out loud and hoped no one heard me. Looking up my gynecologist in the phone book was actually the first step I needed to get the ball rolling. I hadn't been in awhile and needed to discuss with her about tests and a physical. As I dialed the number, I realized that this was really going to happen. The secretary made the appointment and all I had to do was show up. This was it. This was the beginning.

Suddenly, I was afraid. What if... No, I wasn't going to put myself through the what-ifs. I wasn't going to allow myself to think any negative thoughts. I was going to be positive. I was going to put everything into perspective and take proactive measures instead of letting negative things happen and then be reactive to the situation. That was when I felt out of control. Instead, I'm going to take control of the situation and take one step at a time. I'll go to the appointment first and go from there.

I remember driving around the block several times before I realized I was about to be late to the appointment. As I walked in, I suddenly was amazed at how nervous I was about the tests. I had nothing to be afraid of or nervous about, I kept telling myself. I just needed to talk to her and ask questions. She was the only one who knew anything at this point. Besides, who else needed to know anything? This was my decision and no one else's.

Sitting in her office, I searched for my list of questions. I wasn't sure I would get to ask any of them because I figured she would do most of the talking at this point. She was a friendly doctor. I felt comfortable sharing all my thoughts and medical inquiries. She would always answer your questions in a way you could understand. I admired that in her.

As she entered her office, she smiled and asked how I had been and remarked she hadn't seen me in awhile. I told her I was fine, but had some questions I needed answered. For a consultation, she would always take time out of her busy schedule to meet with you for question and answer time. I told her I had made a very important decision in my life, but that I needed some questions answered. My decision was that I wanted to have a child. She smiled and congratulated me. She asked when I wanted to have this child and I told her in June. We talked about possibilities of insemination and choosing a donor. The one thing I had not thought about was who the donor would be. I asked her about the possibility of an anonymous donor. She remarked that there were several sperm banks available if that is what I chose to do. I really didn't have anyone I knew well enough to donate. Perhaps this was the route to go. She told me that first and foremost, I would have to undergo some tests because of my age, familial history of uterine cancer, and genetic make up for twin possibilities. She would schedule the tests and let me know when they were.

Chapter 3

Since I left, I haven't spoken to her. We discussed at one time that her brother would be the donor, because I was going to be the one to carry our child. I wouldn't have trusted anyone else to be the father. Now, I can't seem to fathom anyone else being remotely suitable to be a donor. I don't know anyone here long enough to trust. What I wouldn't give to have her by my side right now. But, since that is no longer an option, I have no alternative but to do this anonymously. I'm not even sure how I feel about accepting a donor I don't know. I'm sure it's perfectly normal to feel this way, but this would not be a normal pregnancy either. So many important decisions to make. I've come this far and I won't back out now.

Besides, it doesn't matter who the father is as long as he meets some sort of criteria. I have to decide what type of criteria. What would I look for in a father-to-be? I guess the same as a *husband*? Let me rephrase that...what would I look for in a *life partner*? I'll know more when I can sit down and discuss these issues with my doctor and she might be able to give me some insight. I just know that this will probably be my one and only chance to have a child and I want to do this right.

I have felt such a freedom from what I once thought were important things in my life. Things like having petty arguments, which don't make sense, spending money on things I don't need, trying to make myself feel better about myself by hurting someone else. All the lessons I've learned from this experience will never be forgotten. I don't ever want to forget this moment. If I had a camera, I would want to take a photograph of my heart and preserve it in time. I want my child to have the sweetest dreams, the once upon a time books, a first kitten, and most importantly, the family he deserves. I suppose most mothers-to-be felt this way. I wonder if mine did.

I wonder if she will want to pass down a few things of mine to him when he is born. I guess now I will be subscribing to all kinds of pregnancy and motherhood magazines which introduces new baby bottles or debating on whether or not breast feeding is best. This is all I have wanted for so long and I have thought of so many names. But, I must remember that I have to take these tests first and get the results analyzed. I just want to embrace this with everything inside of me. It feels right and I want to remember this feeling always. The courage to live and love life has allowed me to take the undiminished risk of all time. I welcome this awesome moment for the right to celebrate, which is the decision to give life. For all the pain and emotion I have endured this past year with losing the love of my life, this new emotion is far more poignant. Starting a new life seems fitting. Perhaps I *have* come full circle.

~

For September, this was one of the coldest days I could ever remember. The howling winds from a

Canadian front swept through the south with a rage of fury. Snow in September is unheard of this time of year. But, accumulation was developing quickly as I headed for my doctor's appointment. She was going to do my tests today. I was nervous but excited as I arrived at her office. Checking in with the secretary, I sat quietly listening to the music overhead. Nothing I recognized, but it was soothing.

Dr. Aubrey Shannon was from Boston, but moved her practice here a few years ago. She had medium, dark hair and dark eyes. Dressed in business casual attire, she always appeared very feminine and professional. I admired the way she approached her patients. She seemed astute and very caring. When I first learned of her practice, I asked around to find nothing but good things were being said about her. Even my mother liked her. I was impressed. I'm glad I had been well informed.

I was eager to discuss my tests and options because I knew she would give me expert guidance. I knew I could trust her judgment as a professional. I just felt comfortable with her as my doctor and knew I could count on her being there for me. Her other patients felt the same and complemented her many times.

As she entered my exam room, she asked how I was doing and if I had any questions. I asked as many as I could remember and she answered them without hesitation. I was amazed at her bedside manner and how comfortable I felt. I wasn't nervous anymore. She began to explain my testing procedure and asked if I was ready and I nodded. As she began the procedure, she asked if I had decided about a donor. I told her that I probably would go with an anonymous donor because I really didn't know anyone well enough or trust as a personal donor. She conceded with a smile and told me to stop by her office after the tests were completed and she would give me some names and phone numbers to call for more information. I agreed to meet with her afterwards.

Just down the hall from the examining room was her office. She had framed degrees and artwork neatly arranged on her walls. Many bookshelves, which housed several medical and research books, were placed behind her desk adjacent from the door. On her desk were pictures of what appeared to be her pet. I sat in a chair just across from her desk and waited for her to return.

As I listened to the music still playing over the intercom system, I thought it sounded familiar to me, but I wasn't sure. I continued to listen as she entered her office. She asked me if I had any other questions and as I sat and thought for a minute, I asked her if she considered me a high-risk patient because of my family history and age. She replied that my age really wasn't a factor but as any doctor would advise, she said that the tests would reveal what was most important. She thought there wouldn't be any difficulties as far as being able to carry a child and having a normal pregnancy, but to be safe we would let the test results speak for themselves. I agreed. She copied down several names and phone numbers for me to call to set up interviews for anonymous donor information. She handed me the piece of paper and told me if I had anymore questions to be sure to call and wrote down an additional phone number on a separate piece of paper, and handed it to me before I left. I put both pieces of paper in my pocket and I thanked her immensely for all she had done.

As I left Dr. Shannon's office I had a wonderful feeling that everything in my life was finally coming together. I had never felt so relaxed or positive about anything in my life. I wanted to tell the world how happy I was at that moment. At that instant I knew I would have to tell my family soon. As soon as the test results came back and the donor was chosen, I would have to face them. I would have to tell my parents they were about to become grandparents and my sisters, aunts. I dreaded the day more than anything, but maybe I could muster enough courage to get me through it.

V.A. Buck

Chapter 4

What was it about a snowy day that makes you want to get outside and enjoy the wonder? I suppose it's the snowflakes and how they intertwine with each other to make a final masterpiece on top of everything it touches. The icicles dangling from the eves of every house in the neighborhood are getting longer by the hour. It's beginning to be a winter wonderland in Tennessee. Its not like we haven't had snow before, but this time of year is unusual. We don't get the snowfalls like the neighboring or northern states.

I remember the snows in Cleveland. The Great Lake Erie, frozen in a white-capped state. People walking out on the frozen lake, setting up camp, and getting ready to ice fish. The winds are brutal blowing off the lake and the snow squalls are both blinding and dangerous when the winds are fierce. You would be lucky to see your hand in front your face at times. Certain areas often getting pounded with snow in the Snow Belt regions, accumulated over sixty plus inches in some counties.

One year, the National Guard being was called in as houses were caving in from snow on top of roofs. The snows were too heavy for the roofs to withstand. The troops were literally bulldozing snow into dump trucks, as they would dump each load back into Lake Erie. It was the only way to get rid of it. But, the snows of Christmas were always beautiful.

Sometimes, I longed for the snows from the north. They are so different from those here. The crunching beneath your feet as you walked along the frozen pavement. The slushy sounds of melting snow as you drove on the highways. The bitter, cold still nights and the sounds of Canadian Geese flying south for the winter were things I would never forget. Ice drenched the trees and power lines during an ice storm and you were afraid to walk outside for fear the limbs or power lines would snap in an instant with a mere footstep. Sometimes, it wasn't uncommon to wake up to fifty-five below zero weather. Your car battery refusing to turn over for a simple drive to the grocery. If you didn't go out every hour during the night to start your car, you could forget it starting in the morning. I remember getting up in the middle of the night to get a glass of water and the pipes would be frozen. Those were cold winters. The snowdrifts were so high that you had to dig your car out. I looked forward to the thawing spring months. The buds of the trees were exploding with greenery, bulbs finally opening to offer the spring colors of reds, violets, and yellows. You knew by then that the winter's cruelty was finally over.

Now, I often wonder if the cold winters are the same...the way they use to be. I suppose it doesn't matter anymore. I will always remember them then. Maybe one day, I'll go back and visit and take my son to see the Great Lake Erie and all of its wonders. Just sit out by the shore and watch the ships come and go, the seagulls following the fishing boats, and enjoy watching the waters crash against the rocks, feeling the spray of each wave. To see the lighthouses beckoning the ships and small boats, searching for the right direction toward land. What small wonders to a child who has never seen the Great

Lake Erie; I would have to make a promise to him to do that. He would never understand my stories if I didn't take him at least once to see it. He would have to know about all the places I've been and the wonderful stories about each place. He would never truly understand me or know who I was without them.

The snow finally stopped and today I would return once more to Dr. Shannon's office. This time, for my results. Finally, this was the day. As I was putting on my winter clothes, I couldn't help but wonder what lie ahead. What she would tell me today would change my life forever and I knew I would never be the same.

The streets were snow-covered as I left for her office. It was peaceful out here, with just the sounds of wildlife or boats racing up and down trying to find the perfect fishing spot. It was difficult trying to keep my mind on my driving. I kept thinking about the results and what she would tell me. Would I be a good candidate for pregnancy? I prayed that I would. I had to keep thinking positive. I had so many emotions that were about to explode. On one hand, I couldn't wait until I heard the news and on the other, I was hesitant. I haven't been able to think about anything else.

Parking the car, my heart started pounding. I walked into the office and checked in with the secretary. I picked up a magazine and started reading when I heard my name called. At that moment, I knew this was it. I entered her office and she was there waiting for me. She asked me to sit and told me we would go over the results together. She told me that all the lab work looked great. Everything was within normal limits of where it should be and that I should be able to get pregnant and carry a fetus to full term. She smiled and asked if I had any questions. I was in shock. I suppose I didn't really expect everything to be this smooth. Subconsciously, I expected something in the lab work to come back not normal. I didn't know what to say. My emotions took over and I began to cry. She asked if I was okay and I just nodded. I told her that I was both relieved and shocked that I was able to have a child. She asked why and I replied that this was everything I had wanted for so long and now it was a reality. She asked if I believed otherwise and I told her I had really been concerned about my age. She said she understood, but as long as I took care of myself, ate right and exercised, both the baby and myself would be fine. She asked me if I had called any of the donor facilities or made any appointments. I told her I wanted to find out first if I was able to get pregnant. Walking out of her office, she placed her hand on my shoulder and told me not to worry, that she would keep me well informed of the procedure, step by step. She told me to call back once I had chosen a donor and we would go from there. I agreed I would call.

As I left her office, I felt at peace. I finally knew I was going to be a mom. After all the questions, dreams, and emotional roller coaster rides, I knew now it would be a reality. All I have to do now is set up the appointment.

Chapter 5

When I got up the next morning, I found the two pieces of paper Dr. Shannon had given me to call. The first piece of paper had three numbers on it and the other had one. I wasn't sure what the number on the second piece of paper was for, but I would call it later. I called the first number and made the appointment. I knew I was pressed for time if I were going to have this child in June. It was already September and that left me the rest of the month to make the decision about a donor and to have the procedure. I had to act fast.

My first appointment was for this morning. I was ready to find out who the donor would be. I knew I wouldn't be able to put a name with a description, because it was totally anonymous. But, I didn't care. I was ready to make a decision today. I knew what I wanted in a donor. The same superior attributes I would also look for in a life partner. I couldn't settle for just anyone. This donor had to be special.

I had to be at my first appointment at nine a.m. The facility was across town and I was thankful I would miss the early morning rush hour traffic. It was a large facility, over twenty stories and my appointment was on the tenth floor. As I entered the crowded elevator, I noticed no one had pressed the button for my floor. So, I pressed the button and the elevator began moving upward, stopping at each floor. As people began getting off and on each of their floors, the elevator became less crowded. I wondered if anyone, excluding myself, was going to the same floor. One more stop and I was there. The elevator finally stopped and I was the only one who stepped out.

I entered the office and gave them my name. The receptionist asked me to complete the necessary forms. She told me the doctor would be with me in a few minutes. As I waited, I contemplated what questions the doctor would ask. I'm not sure it really mattered, but I was curious. I knew I would receive the expert guidance I needed no matter which facility I chose. The nurse opened the door and called my name. I followed her down the hallway into an office. I sat quietly in a chair across from a desk. As she left the room, she closed the door behind her. He soon entered and offered his hand as he introduced himself as Dr. Spalding. I shook his hand and introduced my self as well. He told me that Dr. Shannon had contacted him and he would help me in any way possible. He told me I had several options to choose from and asked if I had considered what I was searching for in a donor. I told him I had several ideas. He handed me a list of all the donors in his facility. He told me I could take the list with me to look over, and if I found one that met my standards to call. I assured him I would.

I arrived home and began searching for the right donor. Scanning the list, I felt I had made the right decision by choosing an anonymous donor. I wouldn't have to worry about any legality assumed by the father. He had waived all rights. I didn't want any lifelong commitment with him, just the child. Besides, the facility didn't accept just any donor. They had to be well screened before they were accepted. I began the search and I was able to dissect the donors one at a time by their description. One that seemed appealing read:

35 year old Caucasian male, 6' 4", 225 lbs., light brown hair, blue eyes; graduate from University of Michigan with a Master's in Engineering; sports enthusiast of golf, water polo, volleyball, baseball, football and tennis.

It seemed the perfect match. I couldn't have written a better criteria list for my child. This was the one. I would call Dr.'s Shannon and Spalding first thing Monday morning.

~

My new life was taking on a whole new meaning. It seemed I had conquered the hardest avenues so far, except telling my family. I promised myself I wouldn't tell them the news until after I became pregnant. Now that it's going to become a reality, I would have to find the perfect place, time and guts to tell them.

I would have to prepare myself for the harsh undertones of all the reasons why I shouldn't have this baby. I decided to have a child, not them. They have no say in the matter. They will come up with a thousand and one reasons why I shouldn't have this child. I just have one reason why I do. Because I want a child. That's reason enough for me.

My youngest sister will applaud me while the other will agree with my parents. Jackie, my younger sister, believes we are so much alike. She approves of my lifestyle and agrees with my analogies. She lives out of state and we stay in touch most of the time. She knows how much I've wanted a child and supports my decision.

My older sister, Gloria, is eccentric and doesn't agree with most of my life decisions or lifestyle. We rarely see each other, except during holidays. It's surprising, because we live in the same town. She's busy with her work as I am mine.

It doesn't matter anyway if they approve or disapprove. I'm simply going to give them the option to participate in his life. It's their choice. When it comes down to the final minutes, I know my family will want to be a critical part in his life. Especially, my parents. They will want the opportunity to spoil him just like my grandparents did me. They will want the special time to teach and love him just like raising there own and it will be a special time for them too, because they want to be grandparents. They thought Jackie would be the first to have a child, but it will be me instead. Gloria never wanted children. She helped raise Jackie from the beginning, so I believe that may have played a critical part in her decision. Nevertheless, my son will have a family if mine chooses not to participate. He will have me. The idea of not having a father, or being married, will all dissipate after he is born; those two issues will be the biggest factors for my parents. They will have to understand that this is my decision and whatever I decide will be best for me and my son.

Today was Saturday and I had some time to reflect on all of this before I contacted my doctor on Monday. I had so much to be thankful for. I was finally healing. I felt as if I was finding myself again. This inner feeling that something great was about to happen in my life felt exhilarating. I felt as if my spirit had been lifted. I knew there would be times when I wouldn't feel so "uplifted", but somehow I knew that my life would be better, more fulfilling, and inspired.

Looking out my window, I watched the squirrels and chipmunks race around gathering nuts. The Blue Jays were making frequent landings to the bird feeder trying to find their favorite feed. It was snowing again and as I watched other birds flying about, I caught sight of what appeared to be a Red Tailed Hawk. I followed its flight to where it had established refuge in an old Squirrel's nest high in an oak tree behind the cabin. As I watched it rebuild the nest, I noticed another massive bird not far away sitting on a dead branch. I wasn't sure what I saw until I retrieved the binoculars. As I suspected, it was the mate. He was guarding her as she started her new home for her baby.

How ironic this was happening. How ironic this hawk had made plans to have her baby here. How had they survived without being sited and killed? What a rare opportunity I had found to watch and learn from such a massive bird of prey. Maybe I really could learn from her in some strange way. Maybe she had been sent here for a reason. The Native American's believed certain animals represented inner spirits. The spirit represented a tribal person in some way. To some tribes, the owl was a sign of bad luck. But to others, it was thought that we could learn about old wisdom, knowledge, paradox, femininity, mystery and vision. The hawk, on the other hand, represented an icon to people who could learn lessons of awareness, insight, truth, adaptability, prayer and openness. This was a good sign. I had truly been blessed with this new awareness. I felt honored in some way that she had decided to nest here. Maybe she was my totem. I always had a keen sense of being able to spot these birds wherever I traveled, and I often wondered if they had been some sort of sign. Maybe she represented my spirit. Ironically, I was born with Native American blood. My Great Grandmother was one quarter Cherokee. I had always been drawn to the legends and folklore of the Indian culture. Perhaps now I understand why. More than ever, I wanted her to stay so that I could observe her and try to figure out what message she would bring. I had an eerie feeling that was her purpose. What could this hawk possibly tell me. I had no idea, but I wanted her to stick around so that I could find out.

Chapter 6

It was finally Monday, and I was ready to make the calls. It was one of those mornings where I found myself getting up and having that passion. The passion to do something right for once. I had longed for that feeling. The feeling that no matter what came my way, I would have a wonderful day. I wished I could wake up like this everyday. Maybe now, I could.

Getting in my car, I looked up and saw the hawk sitting in her nest. What a sight this was...majestic and prominent. I stared at her for a moment as if I wanted her to tell me something. Both her grace and beauty were amazing to me. I had a feeling she knew I was there watching her, but she didn't seem to mind. I almost felt guilty for staring as if I was intruding upon her space and privacy. I started the car and cautiously drove away.

Emotionally, I was ready. I was ready for my own little family. I had learned the lessons of truth, insight, adaptability, and prayer. Openness, on the other hand, was something I needed to work on. It was a trust issue for me. It was because of her I learned to trust again. In the end, I no longer trusted anyone. She told me she would follow me to Tennessee once she found an appropriate job. She never came. To trust again would be something I would definitely have to work hard on. How would I ever learn to trust again? I would need to meet someone very loving and caring and who would understand what I had been through. Where in the world would I ever meet someone like that; certainly not at the local club. It was nothing but a meat market. I was tired of the scene and quite frankly, too old. I promised myself that I would just stay home and become an old spinster with my cats for the rest of my life. But, I wanted a child. What better timing than now? Besides, who needs to go to the club to meet anyone? I wasn't sure I was ready to meet someone new anyway.

This new inspiring avenue in my life to have a child would be more than I could handle right now, let alone meeting someone new and trying to start another relationship. I just wasn't ready for that kind of stress in my life. Timing was everything. Right now, it felt right to become pregnant. That was a priority. It was perfect timing for me. I couldn't help but think how nice it would be to share this dream of mine. The dream that my partner and me would raise my son together, as a family. I wondered if it could only be a dream for me. A dream that two people, in-love, could raise a child. I missed being in love. I missed her. Would I ever get over her? Would I ever stop thinking about the Holy Union we shared and our plans to have a child? Eventually, I suppose I would. I wasn't having second thoughts of having this child, but having second thoughts of ever getting involved again. I had to remain focused on the obvious.

I was heading for work and knew I had to make the two most important phone calls of my life. To call and tell Doctor Spalding that I had found the perfect donor and inform Doctor Shannon I was ready to proceed to the next step. I knew she would help me through this every step of the way. Just the thought of becoming pregnant was something mysterious, yet magnificent. As I arrived at work, I took off my coat and sat at my desk. Picking up the phone, I dialed Doctor Spalding's office. When the receptionist answered, I asked for him. A few minutes went by and then he answered. I told him I had found the right donor and gave the donor's number and description. He was delighted that I had found the right one for me. I told him I would be contacting my gynecologist for the next step and he said he would be in touch with her as well. I hung up the phone and then began dialing Doctor Shannon's office. Suddenly, I realized they weren't open and I quickly hung up, because I didn't want to leave a message with their answering service.

As I watched and nervously waited for an hour to expire on my desk clock, making the call to Dr. Shannon was my next step. I caught myself smiling and realized I was proud of who I had become. I had become my own hero and no one knew that more than myself. Not even her.

I had matured more these past few months than any previous year in my life. I felt proud I had made this decision to become a mother. At one time, I wasn't sure I could've handled the responsibility. I had only wanted to be in a relationship with someone, not ever knowing there could've been much more. But, back then I wasn't ready. Now, I am. Now, I am ready to give all of myself and receive nothing. Isn't that what it's all about anyway? Why had it taken me so long to find that concept, I wondered? Many of my friends I had gone to school with had been married, had children and divorced. I felt fortunate I had not been through that. On the other hand, I guess I had. Even though law did not recognize the Holy Union, I had been married and divorced. I thank God everyday that we didn't have a child together. It would have devastated me to leave the child behind when I came home. Technically, it would have been hers. It would've had her name, not mine, because her brother would've been the donor. Now, I would have a child of my own. This was clearly becoming a reality. I was getting closer to becoming the person I've always wanted to be. People would see me in a different light. Those people who most mattered to me, were my family.

It seems we always want to please our parents, no matter what anyone says, but I also want them to be happy for me. I wasn't sure that would happen, but I felt in time, they would. This was the time in my life where I had to be more honest with myself than I had ever been. I had to realize there would be hills to climb along the way. No matter what, I had to remain both honest and optimistic. There was a child getting ready to come into this world and he would need me more than anything or anyone. I was now ready to step up and take on the challenge. This would be like no other challenge I had incurred. It was time. It was finally time to make that call.

Chapter 7

After the secretary answered, I told her I needed to set up a consultation with Dr. Shannon. She told me she had a cancellation and wanted to know if I could meet with her this afternoon. I told her yes, to set the appointment and I thanked her for getting me in so quickly. I hung the phone and sat for a minute and again realized how quickly things were falling into place. This would be the longest day at work for me in a long time. Monday's seemed to be the hardest anyway, but now counting down the agonizing hours would be the hardest. I couldn't wait to get there and talk about my next step.

More snow was in the forecast and I didn't want to risk being late for my appointment, so as I headed out early it had just started to snow. The weather was forecasting six to eight inches by morning. I arrived without incident and headed in to her office. I checked in and sat in the waiting room, listening to the soothing music overhead. Within minutes, my name was called. Escorted down the hallway, back to her office she was waiting for me. She smiled when she greeted me.

"How is the weather progressing outside?"

"It's just started to snow and they expect us to have about eight inches by morning."

"I had made plans to go up to the mountains for the rest of the week and wondered if the snow would hold off."

"It doesn't look as if it will. But, if you have a four-wheel drive you shouldn't have any trouble."

She asked me if I had one and I remarked I didn't, but I had a front-wheel drive vehicle that pretty much would go anywhere I needed it to.

"How are you feeling about your decisions?"

"I am somewhat nervous, but ready for my next step."

"Do you have any more concerns?"

"I am a really unaware of the facts of becoming pregnant, in the nontraditional way, so how is this going to proceed?" She gave me literature to read and wrote down a web site for me to investigate on my own time.

"Dr. Spalding has contacted me about your choice of a donor and the next step will be to actually set up the procedure to have the insemination. I will have to call the One-Day Surgery Center to establish the surgical procedure."

"Is that really necessary? Why couldn't I have it done here?"

"My office isn't really equipped to do that kind of procedure here. Will that be a problem to have the procedure done at the Center or do you have any preferences as to what day and time you want this done?"

"It would be better for me on my off day, which is either next Wednesday or Thursday."

"It shouldn't be a problem since it was at least a week in advance."

"If you run into any problems, call me at work or home and I will try and reschedule for a better day."

"I will contact you either way to let you know when to expect the procedure and will follow up with you at that time."

I smiled and told her I looked forward to hearing from her very soon. She walked me out to the waiting room and looked out to see the snow had already developed in to a full-blown snowstorm. By the accumulation, it looked as if we would get more than eight inches by morning.

"Do you still plan to make your trip?"

"Yes, I do, but I'm not sure now if I will actually go."

Where she was going would be more snow and worse terrain, but she might reconsider. Being from Boston, I'm sure she knew how to drive in the snow.

"I am a little reluctant to drive when it gets this bad because people around here just don't know how to drive in the snow. We just didn't get that much around here and this time of year was even more of an indicator that people won't be ready for it. Most people used chains because of the mountainous terrain. Some didn't know any better and just used trucks, which resulted in disaster almost every time."

"I would be happy to take you home if you could get a ride later to pick up your vehicle once the snow lets up."

I was shocked by her generosity, but gladly accepted. I knew dad had a four-wheel drive vehicle and he wouldn't mind bringing me back later to get my car. She told me she had one more patient to see and she would be finished for the day.

I agreed to wait for her and sat down in the waiting room. As I waited, I decided to start reading the literature she had given me on artificial insemination and pregnancy. I felt relieved, to some degree, she had given me this to read. I knew it would diminish my ignorance level a notch or two. But, I also had a long way to go to learn everything I needed to go through this pregnancy. I think she too knew this. Now was the time to continue to be honest. I didn't want to assume anything. If I didn't know or wasn't sure, I needed to ask. As I began to settle in and read, she was finished for the day.

"Are you ready to go or do you need to retrieve anything from your car?"

"No, I am ready." We exited out a back door, just down the hall from her office. She locked the door behind us. Outside, I noticed several vehicles in the parking lot and wondered which one would be hers. I envisioned a sport utility vehicle, something resembling a BMW or Lexus. As a doctor, I knew she would have to make a substantial amount of money. And as we arrived at her vehicle, she stopped at a dark burgundy Toyota 4-Runner and unlocked the doors with remote control. I complemented her vehicle and told her that I found it gorgeous. Nothing short of what I expected her, as a doctor, to be driving. I climbed in and closed the door. Inside, all leather, and all the amenities you could ask for in a truck. The vehicle was absolutely spotless. No dust, and shiny as if she just drove it off the show-room floor. Still had that new car smell when you first buy it.

"How long have you had it?"

"Oh, about a year." I glanced over and noticed she had only about fifteen thousand miles on the odometer. I was impressed. She had kept it in great condition. She placed a CD in the disc-changer, shifted into four-wheel drive and off we went.

"Where do you live?"

"I live out on the nearby lake. I'm sorry you have such a long drive to take me home."

"It's really no problem. I'm glad I could help. Do you have any more questions about the procedure?"

"I probably have more questions than your usual patients!" She looked at me with a puzzled look on her face.

"Why would I think that?" I hesitated for a moment.

"It's only because I have never really thought of having a child until the past couple of years."

I wasn't sure where this conversation was going, but I promised myself that I would remain honest. Besides, this was my doctor...I could trust her. I explained to her that I had just come out of a ten-year relationship and we had discussed having a child, but that it never developed.

"Do you have any regrets about not having a child during that time?"

"No, it was probably for the best. I have discovered so much about myself these past few months since returning home from Ohio. I had lost so much of my identity while in the relationship and realized I had given up so much of myself that I had forgotten what I wanted or needed in my life. My family probably won't give me much support in this pregnancy in the beginning, but as time goes by they will soften."

I wondered at this point what she was thinking, but it really didn't matter. She was listening and that's all that mattered to me. She seemed to care. As we drove up my driveway, her tracks were the first. The snow was getting deeper by the minute. I would've never made it in my car.

"Thank you for driving me home."

She smiled and replied, "it was no problem."

I watched her turn around and start to drive away when I saw she had a small rainbow flag in her rear window! I felt my face was flushed as I stood in the driveway, with my mouth open in shock to what I just saw. My doctor, a lesbian? I couldn't believe it. Maybe I only imagined what I saw...a rainbow flag? No, I distinctly saw a flag! Oh my, what a revelation. She was long gone by now and I was still standing in the driveway contemplating whether or not I saw what I thought I saw. The snow was pouring down and I looked like an idiot, I'm sure to my neighbors, standing out there with my mouth wide open! If anyone would have asked what I was doing, I think I would've said I'm catching snowflakes!

I would've never known. I mean, I didn't even suspect. Unfortunately, some are a dead giveaway. Others, you'd never know unless you spotted something like this. Believe me, it's not a bad thing that you might be recognized as one in the community, but being labeled by the community might be. With her credentials, I am amazed that she would even consider letting the community know. Maybe she wanted me to know because she recognized me as one of the community? Should I even acknowledge that I saw the flag?

You know, I shouldn't be so shocked. Being from Boston, it's not so risqué. She's certainly not from the Bible belt! Maybe that's why she's been so accepted. I could care less if she's a *lesbian* or not. She was my doctor and I trust her explicitly. Besides, what difference did it make? It just made it easier for her to understand me as her patient. If anything, I admired her decision to be known in the community. What a statement! That's why I didn't see a picture of a husband, child or family sitting on her desk. I never noticed a ring either...wonder if she was single?

Oh, for God's sake! Who was I kidding? She wouldn't be interested in me...no way! I wondered if that was why she offered to bring me home. I quickly dismissed that thought, embarrassed that my conceit had seeped to the top of my consciousness. I only hoped I didn't say it out loud! I didn't need to be in some twisted, bizarre or whimsical dream. I hadn't even looked at her in that way. I needed to stay focused on my priority. I wasn't ready for another relationship anyway. I was still missing her... Oh well, I suppose the shock would wear off eventually.

All I had to do was show up for surgery, which should be soon. I knew that no matter what, she would take care of me during and after the procedure. Her professionalism would not jeopardize our patient-doctor relationship. Not only was it against the rules, but I wouldn't let it happen. I needed her to fulfill my dream of becoming a parent, not a lover. She was the one that could make it a reality for me. Now, I had to wait one more time for her to tell me that it was all set...all she had to do was name the place and the time, and I would be there.

~

I knew it would be a very long week ahead. It was only Tuesday, and I still hadn't heard anything from my doctor about the procedure. I wondered when she would call. I hated waiting...especially to the last minute. I had to start planning. I was usually a patient person, but this was driving me crazy. I needed to know something so that I could start making arrangements at work. I needed to give them some kind of time line. I would also need to start making arrangements for the baby. I had to start accumulating things for him. So many things to do, it just didn't seem like enough time. I wasn't even pregnant yet, but I felt as if I hadn't enough time to get things in order, just the way I wanted them.

I was just like my dad when it came to things like that. I felt I had to be in control. Sometimes, that wasn't good. On the other hand, when the going got tough or was more complicated than I anticipated, I knew just enough ingenuity to make it happen. I knew I could do it. I worked well under pressure.

This situation was no ordinary pressure. This was about to be the most important and significant event in my entire lifetime. I had to realize that I had nine months to prepare for this occasion. I wondered if that would be enough time. Some people plan years to have a child, while others happen to chance it. I wanted to make sure that I had done my homework and planned well. This was my future, not chance. I knew I would need some help in the planning stages. Maybe the brochures and literature she gave me would offer me the advice I needed.

As I searched for the literature, I ran across the two sets of phone numbers she had written down. I recognized the first piece of paper with Dr. Spalding's phone number. The other piece of paper had only the one number. I wasn't sure who's number had been written down, but I realized it was a local number. Without thinking, I dialed the number. The phone rang several times and then the answering machine picked up and a familiar voice came on the line...it was Dr. Shannon! I quickly hung up the phone and sat down. Holding the phone in my lap, I wondered why she had given me her home phone number. I suppose it was if I had any questions or emergencies. But, isn't that why she had an answering service? I was stumped. Why had she done this? Well, for whatever reason, I wasn't going to assume it was for other reasons. I wasn't going there...I couldn't. I had to keep everything in perspective. I had calmed down enough to get a glass of wine when the phone rang. It was one of those times when I wished I had chosen caller ID on my phone plan, because I really didn't want to answer. But, I decided to answer anyway.

"Hello?" There was a pause on the other line and then I heard it...that familiar voice I had just called a few minutes earlier!

"Did you call?"

I hesitated for a moment and then replied, "yes, I did. One of the reasons I called was, well...because I wasn't sure whose phone number had been written down. I thought maybe...it was another Doctor that I might need to contact, for more information. The other reason I called was because maybe I thought you might have some news for me concerning my procedure."

What a lie, but I hoped it was a good one.

She laughed and then replied, "well, it is another number you can call if you need to."

She was very soft in her tone and I could tell she knew I was nervous.

"You know, it's okay if you need to contact me. Especially, while you are getting ready for this delicate procedure. I realize all of this is new to you and if you ever need to talk, I will listen or answer any questions you might have."

I was amazed at what I had heard.

She said, "the reason I am calling you back is to let you know that I have set up your procedure for next Wednesday, at 8a.m, and it will be at the One Day Surgery Center. Will that work for you?"

Now, I was in shock. I no longer had to wait...

"Yes, it's my day off and that will be fine! Do I need to be there any earlier than 8?"

"No, 8 will be fine and we'll go from there. I have a team that will be ready for you and once you arrive, the surgery center nursing staff will tell you what you'll need to do. You should probably bring your insurance card and picture ID for billing purposes. Also, make sure you have someone to drive you home afterwards. I wouldn't want you to try and drive yourself home."

"How long will the procedure last? I mean, I will need to tell someone how long they will need to stay and wait."

"I would say about three to four hours will be fine. That allows for recovery time too."

"Okay, I will let them know."

"Do you have someone that can give you a ride home after the procedure?"

I thought for a minute and then replied, "yes, that shouldn't be a problem."

I didn't have a clue who was going to bring me to and from the procedure, but I wasn't going to tell her that! I was afraid she would offer and then maybe feel obligated. I knew I would work it out somehow. She didn't need to feel as though I didn't have anyone else who could help me but her. I appreciated her generosity, but she was my doctor.

"Are you sure you'll have a ride, because it's important that you do." I could tell she was serious.

"Yes, I will have a ride...I promise." I hoped I sounded convincing enough to her that she would believe me.

"Well, if your ride has problems driving because of the weather, just call me and I'll come pick you up. It won't be a problem for me."

This was unbelievable! What does she do house calls? Obviously, I wasn't convincing enough. I had to find a way to convince her that I had a ride and she wouldn't need to go out of her way to come pick me up.

"No seriously, I have a ride. I appreciate your offer, but you don't need to do that."

That's really not what I wanted to say, but maybe that would do it!

"Okay, I'll see you next Wednesday at 8a.m. If you have any more questions or concerns, please don't hesitate to call me. That's why I gave you the phone number."

"I will be there at 8 sharp!"

I thanked her for giving me the great news and said goodbye. As she hung up on her end, I found myself still holding my phone. What kind of doctor was she...I mean, do all doctors get this close, or try to, with their patients? I finally hung up the phone, fell back into my chair and just stared at the phone number. What was going on? Was this her way of coming on to me? I promised myself I wouldn't go there... Do I really need to consider her as a possibility? No, I can't do that! I don't know anything about her except that she's my doctor and drives a 4 X 4! I don't see her in that way...that capacity of being anything else but my doctor. Besides, she was the only one who knew what I was about to go through and I want to maintain that relationship. I need her now more than I have ever needed anyone, but only as a doctor. Now, who is going to drive me back and forth from the procedure? That was my next dilemma. I had to find someone I could trust.

V.A. Buck

Chapter 8

Now was the time to call Jackie. I had no other choice but to call her. I knew she would understand and could help me put all of this together before next Wednesday. What would I tell her...everything? This might be the time. I didn't hesitate. I picked up the phone and dialed her number. I was literally shaking as I waited for her to answer. What was I going to tell her...?

"Hello?" The voice was faint and I could barely hear.

"Jackie? Is that you?" We must've had a horrible connection.

"Yeah, is that you Terri?" She sounded awful, like she was sick.

"Are you okay Jackie? Are you sick?"

"No, I'm fine...just got up a little while ago. I haven't had my morning cup of Java or a smoke yet. What's up? Everything okay at home?"

"Yes, everything here is fine. Listen, I need to talk to you about something. Do you have time or do you need to go?"

"Terri, what's going on? You sound really upset or something..."

"I'm okay Jackie, I just need to talk for a minute or two... Listen, I really have to confide in you about something and I need your word that it won't go any further than this phone wire."

"Terri, what in the hell is going on!"

"Okay, calm down. This is what's happening. You know I have always wanted to have a child and now I have the opportunity to do it. No one knows anything except my doctor."

"Terri, that's wonderful! So, what's the problem squister?"

"Well, the problem is...is that...well...

"Just say it Terri!"

"The problem is that next Wednesday, I am going in for my artificial insemination procedure and I'll need someone to take me to and from the One Day Surgery Center. It's because I won't be allowed to drive afterwards. I can't think of anyone to take me or bring me home without telling them what's going on. Can you think of anyone I could ask and trust?"

"Terri, you have a lot of friends there...isn't there someone you could trust enough to call?"

"I really don't think so."

"What about someone from work? Didn't you tell me you have some friends who are "family" you could trust?"

"Well, they are acquaintances...not really friends. I really can't say I could trust them at this point. So, I just don't know what to do Jackie. I am scared to death mom and dad will find out before I'm ready to tell them everything. I can't risk that...not now!"

"Terri, I understand. You have wanted this for a long time. Let me think on it for a couple of days and I'll call you back. Maybe by then, we'll both have someone in mind. Okay?"

"I don't think I can wait a couple of days, Jackie. I'm too wound up and God knows too anal to let this go another minute. I have to figure this out now so that I can sleep! Please help me figure this out."

"Okay, okay...let me think a minute. Listen, you need to calm down. Everything will be okay, I promise. We just have to come up with someone you can trust to tell and take you to the procedure. Well, let me ask you this...

"What?"

"Well, what if you have a taxi pick you up and take you home? I mean, it's a last resort, but it would work."

"Jackie, I think it's an excellent idea! That way, I don't have to tell anyone what's going on!"

"Thank you very much! I knew we would figure this out! Don't you feel better now?"

"Actually, you figured it out! I feel wonderful. Maybe now, I can sleep!"

"Terri, what else is going on? I can tell something's up with you..."

"Nothing is up. Why do you ask?" I wondered what was going through her mind.

"I mean, other than this whole pregnancy thing, everything is fine on this end."

"Somehow I don't believe you squister...I can tell something's up. What are you not telling me?"

"No, I promise Jackie...everything is fine. Really, there's nothing wrong or anything else going on."

I was hoping she would buy in to it. If anyone knew me more, it was my kid sister. We just had this kind of connection where we could tell something was not quite right about the other. We just knew each other that well. Especially over the phone! It was uncanny. It was as if we were twins or something. Jackie was fourteen years younger than me, but we were alike in many ways.

"I'm not buying it Terri! I can tell something's up! Now, spill it! First, let me get a smoke and my coffee...hold on a sec."

Oh hell, what was I going to say now? I couldn't lie to her. What could I possibly tell her that she didn't already know anyway? Besides, she can tell when I make up a white lie. There was really nothing to tell, except for my suspicions. I guess I could tell her the story and get her opinion on the subject. What else was I going to tell her? I had to tell her the truth. Nothing was going on...yet.

"Okay, I'm back. Now tell me what's going on?"

"Do you remember me telling you that I went to my doctor, you know, the gyno? Well, anyway, when I went back to tell her my decision to have the artificial insemination, she gave me two sets of phone numbers to call. Well, I really didn't put much emphasis on those numbers until I tried to call them. The first number was for the donor facility. When I went back for my consultation, I explained to her that I had chosen my donor. We started talking about how bad the weather was progressing and one conversation led to another. The next thing I knew, she was taking me home in the snow! After she dropped me off and was turning the vehicle around, I noticed a small rainbow flag in the rear window of her truck! Oh God, I nearly died... Well anyway, after I went inside, I decided to look for the literature she had given me to read. That's when I found the second phone number she had given me. So, I decided to dial it thinking it would be another doctor I could contact for more information. It wasn't another doctor's number...it was hers!"

"Terri, sounds like she has a lot of interest in you! Are you going to pursue it?"

"Hell no I'm not going to pursue it! She's my doctor and I need her for that purpose and that alone! Are you crazy?"

"No, I'm not crazy! Think about this for a minute... I really think she likes you squister. She is everything you have searched for in a partner. I mean, she's obviously good looking, has a great job, stable, and could give you everything you've ever wanted."

"Jackie, the only thing she can give me right now is a child. She can make that happen for me. I will accept that from her. Anything else, I'm not sure I'm ready for that. You know I still miss Annie and am still hurting. All I can tell you at this point is what's happened. That's all. I will keep you informed about everything, but right now, I have to go. It's been a long day and I need some rest. Okay?"

I hated to cut her off like that, but I just couldn't talk about it anymore. Enough was enough.

"Okay, squister. I'll let you go, but if you need me for anything, just pick up the phone and call me. Actually, call me when you get home from procedure and let me know how things went. Okay?"

"Okay Jackie, I will. Thanks for listening and helping me figure out my transportation dilemma."

"Good luck Terri... Keep me posted on everything with this pregnancy."

"I'll call you as soon as I can. I love you Jackie."

"I love you too."

V.A. Buck

Chapter 9

Wednesday had arrived and it was time. I took Jackie's advice and called the taxi service. I explained my dilemma about the transportation. They assured me it wouldn't be a problem. They would make sure I arrived home safely.

The horn of the taxi was barely audible, but I was glad. It was so early in the morning and I didn't want the sound of the horn to wake my neighbors. As I left for the surgery center, I shut and locked the door behind me. It was a metaphor in some respects. This was a new beginning for me as this day would mark a new page in my life and nothing would ever be the same. It was inevitable. I was closing a part of my life that I knew my family would never understand. Closing the door on living a selfish life and being alone with just my cats. I had so much more to offer. Opening this next door would be a much greater risk. This was it... I could turn around now and forget the procedure. I could, but I won't. This was what I wanted for myself. No one else would have any say in this. I was thirty-nine and I knew the risks. Besides, my doctor assured me I would be okay. She would be there for me no matter what. It was like an *unconditional love,* in a way. It didn't matter to her why I wanted to have a child. It was the fact that I wanted to... period. She could make it happen. That's all that mattered right now. I was going to change my life and I liked what the future held.

Getting in the taxi, I thought of Jackie. I thought of her words over the phone. They consumed me as we drove toward the center. I kept thinking of how she would tell me to calm down and that everything would be okay. I believed that with all my heart...but I was scared. I needed to keep thinking positive. I took a deep breath and sighed. There was no reason to be scared, I thought. I have the best doctor in town. Everything will be fine, I kept telling myself. The taxi stopped and we were there. I gathered my things, paid the driver and got out. I stepped onto the sidewalk and he drove away. I watched as his taillights became more and more dim with distance. Starting to walk toward the door, I wished I had someone to go with me. I felt so alone. No one to share this with...no one to share my joy.

I opened the door and went into the center. I approached the receptionist and gave her my name. She asked me for my ID and insurance card, told me to have a seat and the nurse would call my name when she was ready. I sat down in a chair, picked up a magazine to read when I saw Dr. Shannon arrive through the doors. She didn't see me, but went straight through the set of double doors I knew I would be entering soon. I was really getting nervous. I kept telling myself that there was no need to be nervous...I would be in good hands. The nurse came through the same set of doors, looked at the chart and with a firm voice called out, "Terri Carter?" It startled me for a minute, but then I got out of my chair and walked toward her.

She greeted me with a smile and we went back through the double doors and off to the left to an exam room. She told me to put on a gown and she would be back in a minute. I was glad I had remembered to bring an overnight bag so that I could put my clothes and shoes in it. I got undressed and put the gown on...oh how I hated those gowns. The ones with the backside open... Makes you feel like everyone can see your business. They never do because you're too busy holding the flaps together. The nurse knocked on the door and asked if I was dressed. I told her to come in and she asked if I was ready. Sitting on the hospital bed, I took a deep breath and sighed. I gestured with a nod, laid back and she covered me with a sheet and a blanket. She wheeled me out of the room through another set of double doors and into a small operating room where I saw Dr. Shannon.

The technician started my IV and as I lay there, I watched Dr. Shannon move from one side of the room to the other. I wondered if she would say anything to me before the procedure started. I had started to feel the effects from the drug in my IV when from the opposite side of the room she started walking toward me. Before she put the mask over her face, she looked at me and asked with a smile, "are you nervous?"

I smiled back at her and said, "not any more, now that you are here."

She put the mask over her face and all I could see were her eyes and the shape of her face. She looked back down at me and said, "you know, this is what you've wanted for a long time. I know you will be happy with your decision. It's just like Dr. Joyce Brothers always said, 'it's the salt in the stew that makes it better.' We sometimes need a little spice in life to make things better, don't we?"

I looked at her and suddenly realized I could barely hold my eyes open another second. I felt so relaxed...without a worry in the world. I remembered thinking how I wished I could feel like this all the time. I wanted to answer her but I couldn't. I knew I had to let go and stop fighting the anesthesia.

~

It felt as if I had just awakened from a dream. I was so warm and sleepy, but I couldn't open my eyes. It felt like I was in slow motion. I felt myself drifting in and out of sleep and could hear people around me talking softly. I heard someone ask me if I felt any pain. I tried hard to concentrate, but I was too groggy to answer. It didn't feel like I was in any pain. I felt drunk...but in a good way. It was one of those times where you were glad someone was taking care of you. Now I knew what Dr. Shannon meant when she said I would need someone to drive me home. There was no way I could even sit up at this point. I hoped she wouldn't send me home in this condition.

I felt myself drifting back to sleep when a nurse came by again and asked if I were in pain. I concentrated really hard, but I didn't feel anything. I shook my head and I could feel she was taking my blood pressure with the cuff wrapped around my arm. It was over. The surgery was over, I kept telling myself. "Yes, the surgery is over", the nurse said back to me. I must have been mumbling out loud.

"Dr. Shannon said the procedure went well and she would see you in a little while to make sure you were okay."

I nodded, in hopes she would have recognized my signal. I tried to open my eyes. I wondered if I there was any blood. I finally forced my eyes open and raised up the covers to see if there was anything. The nurse came back over to me and asked if I was okay and I mumbled a question to her about blood.

"You will have some spotting, but nothing heavy. Do you feel any cramps?"

I shook my head and reached for the nurse. I mumbled, "how long did the surgery take?"

The nurse responded, "about thirty minutes. Is there anyone waiting here for you?"

I shook my head and mumbled, "no."

She asked if there was anyone she could call and I just shook my head. I wish someone were here waiting in the lobby for me. It was my decision though. No one could know about this procedure until i was sure i was pregnant. If my family knew what i was doing, i doubt they would've been here. They wouldn't have approved of the procedure anyway because it wasn't natural. The baby wouldn't have been conceived between a man and a woman in a loving way. What i had done was exactly that. A man, i never met, obviously wanted to be involved in the pregnancy. He never met me, but i wanted to have a baby. We just came together in a unique way to conceive a child. At least i hope it worked. Maybe when i see Dr. Shannon, she will be able to offer me some insight about the procedure. I wished she would drop by and check on me so that i can ask some questions. I was just about to drift back into a sleep when i heard a familiar voice. She was checking my chart and asking the nursing staff about me. She walked over and stood to my left side. She had my chart in her hand and i opened my eyes.

"How are you feeling? Do you have any pain?" She wasn't looking at me at the moment. She kept writing in my chart.

"I feel drunk...but a good drunk." She looked down at me when she asked, "are you feeling any pain?" She looked serious.

I said, "is there anything wrong? Did the procedure go okay?"

She smiled and replied, "yes, everything looked good and I don't anticipate any problems."

"You don't expect any problems? What does that mean exactly...that you think it will take?"

"Yes, I think you will become pregnant on this first try because of the ovulation process. In other words, we timed the procedure just right."

"Oh, okay, i understand. I hope you're right."

"We'll let you go home soon...just as soon as you are awake enough to ride home. You do have a ride home, don't you?" I nodded.

"You didn't have anyone in the lobby, so I wanted to make sure you're ride would be here. Do I need to call anyone to come pick you up?"

I shook my head. "I'll call them when I'm ready to be discharged." She looked at me and smiled.

"It won't be a problem for me to give you a ride." I could feel she was reading me like a book. I looked up at her and shook my head.

"You don't need to do that, I'll call a cab. They are expecting me to call them back for a ride home. Besides, that's way out of your way."

"No, it isn't. I'll check back with the nurses in about an hour to see how you're doing. I'll take you home when you're stable." I was too tired to argue anymore. I fell back to sleep.

When I finally awoke, I was in a room alone. It seemed like I was in this same room before they took me in for the procedure. I wasn't as sleepy as before and I was able to keep my eyes open when in walked my nurse. She asked if I was feeling any pain and I again advised her I wasn't. She asked if I was awake enough to get dressed. She helped me sit up on the side of the bed until she was sure I wouldn't be faint. Putting my feet on the floor, I stood up and felt stable. She helped me to the bathroom where I was able to get dressed. I was ready to go home and be in my own bed. I just wanted to sleep. I knew what I was feeling was only temporary and soon I would be ready to go back to work...in a normal sort of way. I wasn't sure how I would feel after the pregnancy really started to take effect. I guess I would know more in about four weeks.

Leaving my room, I stepped into the hallway and asked if I could use one of their phones to call for my ride. The nurse helped me out to the taxi and I got in and sat back. I told the driver to take it easy as he drove and in a few short minutes, I was home. I walked in and sat on the couch and before I knew it, I was yawning miserably and decided to crawl into bed. Forgetting to take the phone off the hook was my first mistake. It rang its normal amount of rings and then the answering machine kicked in. I listened as I recognized Dr. Shannon's voice, just making sure I arrived home safely. The nursing staff must have told her I caught a cab home. I couldn't worry about the repercussions about her taking me home right now. I curled up underneath all my blankets and sighed. I had done it.

It was finally over and all I had to do now was wait for the results. She was very adamant about the procedure and it's timing and felt sure there wouldn't be a problem becoming pregnant. I hoped she was right. I hoped it took on the first try. I wasn't sure I could go through this again if it didn't. It wasn't that the procedure was any big deal, but the emotional struggle, day after day, was such a roller coaster ride that it played havoc on my mind. All I did was worry, like I am now. I didn't want to worry about the procedure anymore. It was over and all I wanted to do was rest. The anesthesia was still in my system and I knew it would be awhile before I could get rid of it. I was glad I was off tomorrow and I could rest before returning back to work on Friday.

V.A. Buck

Chapter 10

It's been four weeks now and I was more tired than I had ever been. I was glad I had my appointment with Dr. Shannon today. I wondered if I was supposed to feel this way. Contrary to popular belief, I hoped not, even if I was pregnant.

I arrived at her office as usual and checked in with the secretary. I sat down in the lobby and waited. Almost falling asleep in the chair, the nurse called my name and i could feel myself struggling to get out of the chair to stand. What was wrong with me I wondered? I've never felt this tired in my entire life. The nurse took me into the exam room and asked me how I was feeling. I told her I felt extremely tired. She took my blood pressure and the rest of my vitals and recorded them in my chart. She told me Dr. Shannon would be with me in just a minute. I sat there, yawning and waited for her to come in and talk to me. I looked around the exam room and noticed several instruments and wondered what each of them was for and if she had used any of them on me. I heard a knock at the door and soon she entered with a big smile and asked, "how are you feeling?"

Without hesitation, I replied, "I'm very tired and keep yawning all the time."

She smiled and said, "that's a good sign! Why don't we go ahead and do some blood work today and see what it shows?"

I agreed and she escorted me out of the room and down the hall where they could draw my blood. She told they should have the results back soon and once they did, she would call for me to come back in. After they took my blood sample, I went home and decided to lie down for awhile. I felt anxious in a way because I didn't know what to expect next. I just felt tired. Was I really pregnant? Was this how I would feel every day now until the delivery? I hoped not as I was about to drift off to sleep, the phone rang. It was Dr. Shannon's office. Dr. Shannon came on the line and said,

"I apologize for calling you so late, but wanted to know if you feel up to dinner?"

"Late? What time is it?"

She replied, "it's eight o'clock, why?"

Wow, I had been asleep for hours and didn't even know I had slept that long.

"Oh, well, I had just fallen asleep as soon as I got home from your office, but I had no idea I had been asleep that long. I haven't had dinner, and I know I need to eat. Can I meet you somewhere?"

"Yes, why don't we eat at Outback? Does that sound okay with you?"

"Yes, that's fine with me. Just give me about thirty minutes to get cleaned up and I'll meet you there."

"That's fine, I'll see you there."

As I hung up the phone, I wondered why I had agreed to meet with her. I wasn't really in the mood and felt so tired. Maybe a good dinner would do me some good, I thought. I got up and started getting myself ready. I could tell I was getting hungry. I wondered what she would tell me at dinner. Would it be a professional and working dinner or would it be a more personal dinner.

Suddenly, I felt myself getting nervous about this. What if... No, I wasn't going there. I couldn't let myself get all worked up over a what-if! It just wasn't fair to me at this point. I couldn't say it wasn't fair of her because she really didn't know how I was feeling at this point about my ex, Annie. I would just have to wait and see how the dinner conversation would go before I could ever say anything. Tonight, I would have to take a good look at her, but in a different way. I would have to see her in a whole new light. I'm not sure I even wanted to... I wasn't sure I was ready to look at someone else in that way.

For ten years, all I ever did was look at Annie in that way. I wasn't sure if it was fair and I wondered if I would feel guilty. Should I feel guilty? Probably not, but she was still in my heart. I wondered if I could ever look at someone else. I'll just go to dinner and see what happens.

~

Pulling into the parking lot, I saw her truck. I got out of my car and started walking through the parking lot and noticed her truck again. There it was...that rainbow flag in the rear window. Oh God, I need a drink! I felt nervous all over again. What would Jackie tell me to do at this point...probably to take a deep breath and let it out, slowly. I tried that, but it didn't seem to help. My stomach was already in knots as I started to walk in to the lobby. I stopped at the hostess desk and asked where Dr. Shannon was seated. She stepped away from the podium and began to escort me to her table. We walked toward the back of the restaurant and over to the right, where she sat. She was dressed in blue jeans with a white, long sleeve v-neck sweater. I had never seen her wear blue jeans before. She was always dressed in a professional manner at her office. She had dark skin and she always looked as though she had a tan. The sweater made her look even more tanned; much like her white lab coat did from her office. I noticed the gold hoop earrings she always wore at the office and how it offset her dark skin and hair. She was looking at the menu, so she didn't see us coming at first. As we approached the table, she looked up and smiled.

I thanked the hostess and slid in the booth, sitting across from her. I had to admit she had a pretty, white smile. I could only wonder what was going through her mind!

"I hope you haven't been waiting too long. I got ready as quickly as I could."

"No, I haven't been waiting that long at all. Actually, I just got here about five minutes ago."

"Good. So, do you have any news for me about my blood work?"

"Yes, I actually do and that's one of the reasons why I wanted you to meet with me. The blood work showed something interesting, but nothing for you to be alarmed about. Dr. Spalding called me with some interesting data regarding the donor you chose. It seems that every person who has chosen this same donor has given birth to twins. The most interesting fact is that most have been...well, twin baby boys."

"What are you saying? Are you saying that I am going to have twins?"

"Well, we aren't positive at this point, but what I can tell you is that you are pregnant."

"Wow. I'm pregnant? I'm actually going to have a child? Maybe twins? Oh my...I'm not sure I'm ready for...twins. Are you sure it's possible?"

"According to the data, you could very well wind up with twins. We won't know any more until a little further down the road as to the sex of the child and whether or not you would have twins. Are you disappointed?"

"No, not really. I mean no...I'm not disappointed at all. I guess, I'm shocked. I never even considered twins as a possibility. Are you sure?"

"Yes, it's a possibility. Terri, don't worry. I'll keep you informed every step of the way. We won't know more for four to eight more weeks. We might be able to hear two heartbeats. We won't know the sex of the child until probably your second trimester. So, until then, don't worry."

"What should I tell my family?"

"That's entirely up to you. To be honest, I would just tell them that you're pregnant at this point. Anything else would be just a guess. What do you want to tell them?"

"Well, I know they won't be happy at first when I tell them I'm pregnant because I'm not married. But, as time goes on, I believe they'll come around when they realize this will be their *first* grandchild. I'll have to tiptoe around the subject for a little while."

"I know it's up to you, but if you need to talk or need any advice on the subject, I'm here."

I felt comfortable talking to her about this. She was probably the only person i had to talk to, besides Jackie. The waitress approached our table and asked if we were ready to order. I looked at Doctor Shannon and asked shyly, "I guess a drink is out of the question?"

She laughed and said in a matter of fact way, "yes, I'm afraid so!" I asked the waitress to bring me a sweet tea and she ordered water with lemon. I studied the menu and made a choice for the ribeye steak and as i looked up she was watching me.

"What?" I asked, as I my face became flushed. Whenever I get a little uncomfortable or embarrassed, I can feel my entire neck start to get red and then it moves up through my face and out to my ears!

"I just wondered what you were going to have for dinner? Are you okay?"

"I'm sorry, I'm fine. It's just that all of this is a surprise to me."

"All of what? The pregnancy, twins, or us meeting for dinner?"

Oh boy, I could feel my neck starting to get red. What in the hell was I going to say now? I could tell her the truth...but I could omit the last part of me being surprised she asked to meet me here for dinner. My ears were blood red by now, but I had to tell her something.

"Well, I'm actually glad you asked. Why else did you ask me to meet you for dinner, besides to tell me the results of the blood work?" I had avoided her question by asking her a question in return. I was actually curious.

"I asked you to dinner to not only tell you the results of your blood work, but to also spend some time with you...because I want to. I have been curious about you for a long time. As a matter of fact, since you first became my patient several years ago. I had just moved here from Boston and didn't know anyone. But, then you stopped coming in and I didn't know what happened to you until you returned a couple of months ago. When I say I'm curious about you, I mean I want to get to know you as a person and not just as my patient. Also, let me be the first to tell you that I don't normally meet with my patients like this...this is a first for me. I think it's highly unethical to become close with my patients."

"Close?" I asked in a curious manner.

"Well, yes...close." I watched her closely while she struggled for the right words to say. The waitress brought our drinks and asked if we were ready to order. What a great time for this conversation to take a break!

"I'll have the ten ounce ribeye, baked potato with butter and sour cream and on my salad, no croutons and add blue cheese dressing."

"Well, that sounds good. I'll have the same."

The waitress thanked us for our order and she walked away quickly. Sitting there, across from her I could feel she was getting a little uncomfortable. I studied her face, searching for some sort of answer. But there was nothing I could read in her face. I didn't want her to feel uncomfortable, so I nonchalantly said,

"I wondered where in Boston you lived. I have a friend that use to live on the west side of Boston, near the hospital I think." She folded her napkin in her lap and looked at me with curious intent.

"I lived on the east side, near the cathedral and worked at the hospital on the west side."

"I've never been to Boston, but I hear it's beautiful in the fall. In fact, I've never been to any of the New England states, but I've always wanted to go. There's so much to see historically."

"Getting back to the subject, she said as she smiled. I will always be your doctor, but I want to get to know you on a more personal level. Terri, I am very attracted to you..."

I stared at her, struggling for the right words to say and if ever there were right words, now was the time! I felt more nervous now than I ever had in my entire life! I wanted to crawl underneath the table and hide. I looked at her and stared into her dark eyes, searching again for answers.

"You know, I have just come out of a ten-year relationship. I know I probably need to be around more women and start dating again, but I still miss her and I still think about her; but not in a romantic sort-of-way. I guess I just don't have any closure yet. I really never thought I would be having this kind of conversation again with another woman, either. Do you like this area and do you plan on being here for awhile? I mean, I've just relocated back to this area from Ohio and I'm not looking to move away again."

She folded her hands in front of her and studied my face. I could feel her eyes looking into mine as if she were watching for cues. I leaned forward, closer into the table.

"Well? Do you plan on moving your practice?"

She smiled when she said, "I'm sorry, I thought your question was rhetorical." I smiled and sat back.

"You know, when I first moved here from Boston, I had just come out of a relationship, too. It wasn't as long as yours, but it was close enough in years where it wouldn't make much of a difference. I think moving here was my closure. I knew I needed to get away to survive. Her name was Katie. She was an alcoholic, abusive and had grown up in the same type of atmosphere. I knew if I didn't leave, some day I might not be able to. I don't know why I stayed in the relationship as long as I did, but I am thankful I had enough strength to get out. Not only did that save my life, but my career. She was also a doctor and many of our friends were worried she would have some sort of breakdown if I left. Sometimes, I will get emails from my friends and colleagues in Boston telling me about how she is doing. They say she has been in AA and doing well. Of course, that's been several years ago since I left and no matter how much I struggled over that decision, it seemed it was the right one. Now, I know it was for her. We both needed to turn our lives around and by my leaving, we were both forced to do that. I have a wonderful practice here now and I have no reason to return to Boston to live. I'm not from there anyway. I was actually born in Germany, but I was raised in New York after my father was transferred stateside from the Army. I grew up in Queens. But, enough about me, what about you?"

Wow, I had no idea she had been through such an ordeal. How could anyone abuse her in any way? She was very soft spoken and caring. I wondered what type of abuse she had endured. Maybe one day, she would confide in me. She was already confiding in me about her situation and the least I could do was the same. I wasn't sure I could, but i had to try. It was one of those moments where I knew I had to put on a face and act as though it didn't bother me to talk about her...

"Her name was Annie. She was very athletic and had one day planned to compete in the Olympics. We actually met here and when she completed her Master's degree, she wanted to move closer to her family. I agreed to leave my friends and family to be with her. Like every couple, we had our problems. She was from the north and me from the south. We were as different as night and day, but we were drawn to each other through our differences and needs. She had been in an abusive marriage for about two years and knew she had to get out to survive. I wasn't her first, but second. I was living by myself, out in the country in an old farmhouse by the river and she was intrigued that I could do that. She'd never lived on her own before and knew she couldn't. I had what she wanted. The ability to live on my own and take care of myself, both financially and physically. My family was not impressed with her because she was so out-spoken. Being from the north, it's just the way most express themselves. I knew we were in trouble from the start because my family didn't like or appreciate her for who and what she represented. I should've known then, but went anyway because of how I felt about her."

I could feel my heart pounding when I finally stopped talking about her. At least I didn't cry. It was clear I was hurting, but I didn't want her to see that in me. Besides, I hadn't been through the physical abuse she had endured, but somehow the emotional scars felt just as bad.

The waitress finally brought us our food. We sat for a minute in silence as we started eating. She looked at me as if she wanted to ask me something personal. I could tell she was curious about something, but she didn't say anything. Finally, putting down her fork, she looked up at me and in a whispering voice she asked, "why did you come back here instead of staying there in the area?"

I thought about the promise Annie had made to me about following me to Tennessee once she found a good job.

"Annie promised me she would move here once she found the perfect job in her career field. But, she never planned to as I found out later. It was just a plot to get me to move out."

"Why didn't she just ask you to move out, if she wanted you to go?"

"Because she knew I wouldn't leave. I was committed to that relationship and to her, no matter what."

She just looked at me and shook her head.

"Was I stupid or what?"

"No, that's not what I was shaking my head about. You just don't find people like you anymore who are so committed to the relationship the way you were. I mean, you were willing to sacrifice everything to move up there for her and then she wouldn't move back here for you."

She was right. I had never looked at it that way before. She obviously didn't love me enough to do that. What a revelation!

I looked at her and said, "you know, you're right. I had never looked at it that way before. How had I not seen that? I guess I was too much in the middle of it all to see anything. I have been blaming myself for the relationship failing."

We continued to eat our meals and praising the chef as we took each bite. I was amazed at how much food I was eating. I guess it seemed appropriate, since I was eating for two now. But, as far as this conversation was concerned, I was comfortable with what I had revealed. I was blatantly honest and for a change, it felt good to be open about Annie. I wanted to be honest with her. I had no reason not to. But more than anything, I wanted to know more about her. I put my fork down and leaned back. She had obviously been finished with her meal before me and she was watching me.

"How about some dessert?" I rolled my eyes and shook my head in an instant.

"No way...I'm too full! Why don't you have something?"

"I think I'll have a piece of silk chocolate pie!"

Oh God, a woman after my own heart! She likes chocolate! I smiled and nodded in agreement. Our waitress brought her the pie and I sat and watched her in awe. How could I be so lucky to have a wonderful doctor and a new friend? Maybe, a new relationship.

She picked up her fork and carefully pierced the end of the pie, making sure to get all the way through the crust. Then, she offered me the first bite. I looked at her, smiled and accepted. I reached for the fork, but she didn't want me to take the fork from her. Instead, she wanted to feed it to me. I leaned in toward the table, open my mouth and she slowly fed me the first bite. I watched her as I chewed slowly, wondering what in the world was she thinking! Her eyes were fixed on my mouth, as if she wondered what it would be like to kiss me. I could feel my heart pounding and I wanted to ask her what she was thinking when our waitress returned to our table, asking if there was anything else we needed. I blushed and looked away. The waitress left the bill and was about to turn away when she said, "I hope you have a 4-wheel drive because the snow is really coming down out there!" We looked outside and sure enough, it was pouring. I looked at her and laughed when I said, "I might need a ride home?" She smiled back and winked, as if to say yes. She finished her pie and we settled up with the bill. We each climbed into her truck and left the restaurant.

Chapter 11

Pulling up the driveway, the snow had completely covered everything. The trees were accumulating the wet snow by their branches and were weighing heavy by the hour. Power lines also had a thin coating and were beginning to droop. Even the chimney had a layer of snow that had made a sharp outline of white against the painted edges. The birds were flying to and from the bird feeder, filling their bellies with every morsel. As I watched them flying aimlessly about, I heard a familiar screech and smiled. I knew the mother hawk was around. I looked at her and asked her if she would mind getting out so that I could show her something. She quickly turned off the engine, and almost instantaneously, there was silence. All you could hear was the snow falling. I looked up and spotted the hawk in her nest. I took her arm and led her in the direction where the hawk could be seen best and then pointed upward toward the nest. She cupped her hands above her eyes, so that the snow wouldn't hinder her sight. She turned to me, "is that what I think it is? A hawk?" I smiled and nodded in delight.

"Actually, it's a Red Tail Hawk. She's been nesting here only a few weeks now. Her mate is around here somewhere."

She continued to watch when the mother hawk decided to spread her wings. It was as if she knew we were watching her and wanted to give us a regal display of her massive but graceful abilities. We watched her fly down from the nest and right over us until she was out of sight. It was getting darker by the minute and I knew she needed to go before the storm set in. I thanked her for bringing me home and we started to walk back to the truck. She opened the door and then stopped. Turning around, she started walking toward me. My stomach turned a flip, unaware of what would happen.

"You know, I think you are the better person for returning home. She is the one who has lost, not you."

I felt my eyes start to swell up with tears, but I smiled and nodded in agreement. It was all I could do not to cry. She put her arms around me and held me for a moment, as if she were apologizing for her comments.

She pulled away and looked at me, "I didn't mean to make you cry. I just wanted you to know that you are the stronger person, not her." I could feel the tears begin to flow down my face. She took her fingers and wiped them away as each fell.

"I'm so sorry." She put her arms around me once again and held me for what seemed an eternity. I held her tightly. I felt safe in her arms. She was the first person I had released all my feelings to, hoping she would understand...and she did. She released her grip and pulled away slightly looking at me with a look of concern. Standing there, I looked at her with tears in my eyes and for a moment I was sad. She took her hands and put each one behind my neck and pulled me in close to her. She leaned toward me and put her lips on mine. Ever so slight, a warm kiss. I felt her sigh as she kissed me. My heart skipped a beat as she pulled her lips from mine and turned away. As she walked toward her truck, I was amazed at how I felt. I didn't want her to go... I couldn't say a word. She got in her truck and closed the door.

I watched her drive away with that old familiar feeling in the pit of my stomach. I didn't want to admit she'd made me feel something. Still standing in the driveway covered in snow, reality kicked in and I headed for the front door. I walked inside and closed the door behind me. I grabbed a bath towel from the bathroom and began drying my hair. Looking in the mirror, I wondered what she was feeling or what possessed her to kiss me. I remembered how warm her lips were against mine. I closed my eyes and felt that feeling again, as if she just kissed me. It was our first kiss.

V.A. Buck

Chapter 12

As Aristotle once said, *"the only thing that's permanent is change."* I could feel my life beginning to change and take on a whole new meaning. I had no reason to procrastinate now about the pregnancy or my baby. I had to tell my family. I had to break the news to them in a way where it wouldn't be a bombshell. But, how? How would I face them and my fears at the same time? I had to find a way to do both. If I failed to tell them in the beginning, it would only make things harder as I grew near the delivery date. They would be excited about having a grandchild by then, but only if I told them now.

I was about five weeks pregnant by now and that's all I knew. That's all I could tell them. Since my mother had worked in an obstetrician and gynecology office, she would probably understand more at this point than dad would. I had a slight edge because at least she liked my doctor. Anyone else and she would probably try to get me to change. That's just how she operates sometimes. I wasn't sure how she would react, but I had to tell her first, then she would tell dad. There was no sense in calling a family meeting and then having everyone pass out, all at the same time! I needed to do this in a small and calm way, but memorable. Knowing my family the way I do, they will all be in shock for awhile. I had to remember that this was my choice and no one else's. I was giving them an opportunity to be a part of my child's future. All I had to do was find the courage to have the conversation.

Since my mother was retired, she would be at home more and I would be able to have the conversation with her in private. She would feel more comfortable anyway in her own home. Me, on the other hand, I would feel totally out of control and like I was fourteen again! I had to remember I was a grown woman and having a child was what I wanted to do at this time in my life. Who was I trying to convince, me or her? It didn't matter, that's how I felt. No, I didn't know everything, but she could help me understand things. I needed my mother during this period. I needed her support, much like the support of Dr. Shannon. I needed to tell mom how much I needed her and her support.

After given this discussion much thought, I decided I would call mom and see when she would be home. I was tired of prolonging the agony of how she and the rest of my family would react. It needed to be out in the open, and frankly, I was excited about the fact that I was going to have a baby! I hoped she would be, too.

"Mom? Do you have any plans for later this evening?"

"No, but your father does. I believe he has a meeting at church. Why?"

"Well, I just wanted to make sure you would be there if I dropped by for a few minutes."

"Sure, I'll be here…is there anything wrong Terri?"

"No, not at all. I was just going to be in the neighborhood and wanted to stop by."

"Have you had dinner dear? I could fix you something if you're hungry. We had roast for dinner and have some left over."

"Yes mom, I've already eaten, but I might take some with me? I should be there within the hour, okay?"

"Okay, dear...I'll see you in a little while."

Driving over to 15th Street, I began to feel the emotion. The emotion that i had to tell them the worst possible news. It's how you feel when you dread to tell your parents you've wrecked the family car! I shouldn't feel this way, I know. This should be the happiest moment in my life...and it really is...so, why am I feeling like this? Probably because I know how they are going to react! Well, I was almost there. Just a few more turns...there's the driveway. I almost felt like I was going to be sick. Oh God, I dread this! Just stay calm...you can do this, I reminded myself. I rang the doorbell and mom came to the door and let me in.

"Hi mom. How was your day today?"

"I'm doing great today honey, how was yours?"

"Actually, not bad at all. I've had a pretty good day."

"Why is that dear? Were you off today?"

"Yes, I was off today, thank goodness. These hours are about to take a toll on me. I'll be glad when we get back on a normal schedule of eight-hour shifts instead of ten."

"Those are hard hours, I know. When I worked at the hospital years ago, they had us on those types of rotating shifts. With you girls growing up, it was especially difficult because you're father was also working and going to school. We hardly saw each other."

"Speaking of which, I need to tell you something."

"What is it dear?"

"You know we've had the discussion about the biological clock, mine to be more specific. I realize that my age might have a lot to do with that, but you also know I've wanted a child for quite some time now."

"Yes, I know...we've had more discussions about that than I care to admit. It's just your clock ticking dear, that's all."

"Well, I know that it's ticking. I've been to see my gynecologist, Dr. Shannon, and she thinks I would be a good candidate to become pregnant. You remember Dr. Shannon?"

"Yes, when did you go see her?"

"Actually, I've seen her several times since I have moved home. We've spoken in great lengths about my health and my body and if I would be able to carry a child to full term. She believes everything would be fine."

"Fine for what? Having a child?"

"Well, yes to have a child. What did you think I was talking about? Listen mom, I have to tell you this because...

"Because you want to have a child, I know."

"Yes, and I'm going to have a child. How do you feel about being a grandmother?"

"A what?"

"A grandmother...yes, you are going to be a grandmother in nine months...actually, make that eight months."

"You're pregnant? But how? I mean, with whom? I mean, whose is it? Do I know him?"

"Slow down mom...let me start at the beginning. Okay? I had a procedure done about five weeks ago...artificial insemination. I chose someone from the local facility, and no, you don't know him and neither do I. This was the route I wanted to go."

"You mean to tell me that you went to a 'sperm bank'?"

"Yes, mother, I did. I don't want a husband, just a child. I want a family of my own. Can you understand that?"

"Yes, but there are ways of doing that where you wouldn't have had to go to a 'sperm bank'. Just the thought of that repulses me!"

"Mom, listen, I could have adopted a child of my choice, but I wanted to experience the whole feeling and emotion of motherhood. I wanted to know how it feels when the baby kicks and turns over and all that. I wanted to experience each trimester at a time. I can't tell you how happy I am about this... I am experiencing things only privileged women can. My whole outlook on life has changed! And yes, it's because I'm pregnant and I'm finally going to have a child. It's all I've wanted for so long. I don't need anything else in my life for myself, but this child. Can you understand that?"

"Wow, you really are pregnant. You're actually going to have a baby. I'm going to be a grandmother for the first time. I can't believe it..."

"I know you must be in shock... I know you didn't ever expect me to be the one to give you a grandchild. But maybe not only one...maybe two."

"What are you saying? You might be having twins?"

"It's possible, mom! I won't know for sure until a few more weeks. Even then, I'll probably know if I will have a boy...if not sons. They have collected the data from the same donor I chose weeks ago. Every person, so far, has had twin boys. What do you think about that?"

"All I have ever wanted for you girls is to be happy. For the first time in a long time, I can see how happy you are. I don't think I've ever seen you this happy! Look at you! You are actually glowing...that's a look I remember. Being pregnant with you girls made me so happy. I understand how you feel right now."

"So, you're not mad?"

"Mad? Why would I be mad? Listen Terri, you are a grown woman and can make decisions on your own. I might not agree with the decisions my daughters make, but it doesn't mean I will be mad. I try to understand why each of you make the decisions you do, but this one is simply the best decision *you've* ever made! I am so proud of you!"

"I am so happy mom... I'm glad you understand and approve. I was so afraid you wouldn't understand or even want the chance to know your grandson. I need you mom. I need you more now than ever. There are so many things I'm unaware of and unsure about with this first pregnancy. Will you help me?"

"Of course I will! Just let me know anytime if you need anything. I'll be here for you."

"Listen, what about dad and Gloria?"

"Let me handle your father and your sister, Terri. Don't worry another minute about them. I'll take care of it, okay?"

"Okay mom...I'll let you do all the talking. How do you think dad will take it?"

"He'll be fine, I promise. Once I remind him that he will be a grandfather for the first time and she will be an aunt. They'll both understand."

"Are you sure, mom?"

"Yes honey, I'm sure. By the way, have you told Jackie yet?"

"No, actually I haven't. I'll give her a call in the next day or so, okay?"

"Okay. Let me know if you need anything. Let me fix you some of this roast to take home with you. You'll need your strength, especially if you are feeding two now! I can't believe you might be having twins! This is so exciting Terri!"

"Well, I'm not sure how I feel about having twins yet. I only wanted one, but if it turns out that I'm having two.... Then, so be it. I'll deal with it. I just feel so blessed that I'm pregnant. Did you ever feel that way?"

"Of course I did! Like you, I wanted to be pregnant. I couldn't wait until I became pregnant. When do you go back to the doctor for your check up?"

"I'm not sure, I think in about four weeks...hopefully, I'll know more then if I'm having twins or not. She said they would probably be able to tell by then. I'll keep you posted, I promise."

"Here's your roast. Now, if you need anything else, don't you hesitate to call me Terri. You hear me?"

"I will mom. I'll see you later and if I hear anything, I'll call."

I waved goodbye and shut the door behind me. I was so glad that's over with! I am shocked that it went so well. Maybe I misjudged her and the rest of my family. We'll see how dad and Gloria take the news. Mother said she would handle it though, so I'll let her.

V.A. Buck

Chapter 13

I was now in my twelfth week and due to see Dr. Shannon. I really wanted to see her again. I wanted to talk to her more about my pregnancy and what we discussed at the restaurant. I hadn't forgotten about the kiss either...

With all that was happening with me and telling my family, I guess I had put things on the back burner for a few weeks. I didn't want to do that, but I really didn't have much choice. Maybe now was the time for me to progress forward and start to date again. She would be the only one I would ever consider right now. I felt comfortable with her as my doctor, too. I knew I would have to confront her about this sooner or later. My appointment with her was today, so what better day than today. Besides, I had plenty of questions to ask her about the pregnancy and I would just throw in a question here and there about the other night. What could it hurt? If she weren't interested, I would know by now! I think Jackie was right about that.

Jackie seemed to be right about everything lately...especially about me. We just had that special connection between sisters. Too bad Gloria and I aren't like that. It was her choice to exclude me from her life because she didn't agree with my lifestyle. She doesn't know me anymore. That's okay, she'll eventually come around. Anyway, I think I'll give Dr. Shannon's office a call to make sure my appointment is today. I seem to be absent minded lately. It must be the pregnancy.

"Hi, this is Terri Carter...I think I have an appointment today, but I can't remember what time."

"Let's see, Terri...yes, you do have one today at 3:30...is there a problem?"

"No, not at all...I just couldn't remember what time it was scheduled. I'll see you then."

I hung up the phone and looked at the clock and saw it was just enough time for me to take a shower and drive across town to make it there on time. Thank God it wasn't snowing!

I felt really bloated today for some reason. Undressing for my shower, I realized why I felt so bloated. There it was...I had started to show already. No wonder! Rubbing my belly seemed to give me some comfort. It was hard for me to imagine that there was really another human being growing inside of me. How insane that sounded to me. I wondered if my mother felt the same way when she found out she was pregnant? No matter how crazy it sounded, this was the most important decision I had ever made in my life. I would see more changes in my body soon and I had to be prepared for what was about to transpire. Even after reading some of the literature Dr. Shannon had given me, I knew some of those changes would make me feel uncomfortable, but I could deal with them. It was worth all the changes I would go through.

Letting the water from the shower beat down on my belly felt soothing. I agonized for a moment over how big my belly was going to be. But then as I continued to rub in a circular motion, I somehow knew that this tiny human being inside of me would be worth every struggle, every pain and every sacrifice I went through.

My clothes weren't fitting well anymore, so I struggled as I searched to find something a little loose around the edges. My jogging suit would work for now until I could find something more suitable. Just enough elastic to fit, but not binding! I knew that wouldn't last long! Grabbing my jacket, out the door I went. I hated to be late for anything, but this was a really important day. I had to see her. I couldn't wait to get there... I wondered if she would be as excited to see me as I would be to see her. I hoped we would be able to talk privately, but maybe it wasn't the right place to do that. I just didn't know yet how she felt about those kinds of things. She seemed to be open-minded. I would know more once I got there and saw her. I wanted to see her reaction to me. I hadn't even spoken to her in over four weeks. Maybe she changed her mind about me by now. I couldn't even fathom that possibility! Surely she knew my appointment was today. I wondered what would be going through her mind. I wondered what she thought about the kiss.

Driving down the road, Pachelbel's *'Canon in D'* began to play. I listened to each piece and felt more relaxed within minutes. I knew I would soon be there and had to prepare what I would say to her about that night. I wasn't sure, but I knew it would all be good. How to say things just right was not my best suit, but I would try my best to come across in a manner she would know I was pleased. How did I feel? I wasn't sure, but I was curious enough that I wanted to know more about her. I definitely wanted to have more dinners and conversations with her. I probably should ask her over for dinner. That would at least let her know I was still interested. I wasn't sure where I wanted this to go...I wouldn't know that for awhile. She knew where my heart was anyway. Unfortunately, still in Ohio. But, all that could change if the right person came along. Was she the one? I didn't know I thought, as I pulled into the office parking lot. Well, this was it. Just take a deep breath and let it go. "Relax," Jackie would tell me. Where is my sister when I need her? It didn't matter now, I was here.

Getting out of the car, I felt a pull in my belly and I froze. I told myself, I was at the right place if anything was wrong. Slowly, I made my way to the front door and checked in. I sat down, but I didn't feel anything else. I guess I was okay. I didn't feel any more pulls. Maybe I just got out of the car in a weird angle or something.

"Terri? The doctor will see you now."

I got up slowly and again, nothing. I was relieved. She escorted me once again down the hall and into an exam room. I undressed, put on the gown and sat on the table wondering what I would say. She finally entered my room and I looked up at her. As usual, she was smiling. What a relief! I was so afraid she would have a different attitude toward me for some reason...maybe she didn't think the kiss was all *that*...

"How have you been feeling these past few weeks? Do you still feel tired or run down?"

"Yes, I feel a little tired, bloated, and I can't remember anything!"

"All par for the course! Lets see if we can hear a heartbeat today, shall we?"

"Do you think we might be able to today? I mean, I thought it might be too early yet."

"Let's see what we can hear or see...it's called an ultrasound. Now, just lie back and I'll just put some of this gel on your belly and see if we can detect anything. Okay?"

She took the hand-held device and placed it on my belly and began to move it slightly.

"Well, what do you see? Anything yet?"

"Terri, look closely...right there. Do you see it? That's your baby right there."

"I don't see anything...where is it?"

82

"It's resembling a peanut. I'll print it out for you so that you can study it more closely when you get home.

Let's see if we can hear a heart beat...hold on and let me turn on the speaker so you can hear it too. This is called a Doppler device. It will allow us to hear the heartbeat." She placed it on several areas on my belly and listened very carefully. She kept searching, ever so slightly, inch by inch until finally I heard something that reminded me of a kitchen timer, only more faint. I watched her closely listen to the rhythm. She looked at me and smiled when she said, "hear that? That's the baby's heartbeat! And, I only hear one. Doesn't look like twins."

"My God, it's flying! Is that healthy for it to be beating that quickly?"

"Yes, it usually beats about 120-160 beats per minute now. It's still pretty early, but don't worry, we'll keep a close eye and ear from now on, until you deliver...which should be around June 26th."

"Well, at least I have a due date now. I told my mother yesterday. She took the new pretty well. Actually, I was very surprised how well she did take the news. I told her I was very happy and had a whole new outlook on life. She told me she could see how happy I was."

"I'm glad you are happy. Is there another reason why you are so happy?"

She looked at me the way she always does. Maybe that's why she does it so often. She proceeded to clean off my belly and waited for my response. I kept watching her...but she never looked directly at me. Finally, I thought I better say something now or I would regret it...

"Dr. Shannon..."

"Please Terri, call me Aubrey." She handed me my print out of the ultrasound and began to smile.

"Okay, Aubrey...yes, I am very happy we were able to finally get together and go out to dinner. I also enjoyed our conversations. I just really enjoyed your company. I really enjoyed our time we had at the restaurant and... afterwards."

"Afterwards?"

"Well, yes afterwards when you gave me a ride home during the snow storm? I pointed out the Red-Tail Hawk to you and..."

She still had not looked directly at me.

"Yes, I remember...I enjoyed your company too and would like to see you again soon... "

"As a matter of fact, I was thinking the same thing on the way over...how about letting me cook dinner for you? What are some of your favorite foods?"

"I enjoy Italian, Mexican, grilled chicken, steak, burgers...I'm pretty flexible."

"That gives me quite a bit to choose from...how's this Friday evening sound...say, around sevenish?"

"I'll be there...anything I can bring? How about a bottle of White Zinfandel?"

"Sounds great! My favorite! I'll see you at seven..."

She left the room wearing that same smile and I was left to get dressed...

Chapter 14

I was one of these people who didn't like to follow written directions, but rather try to figure it out by a hands-on approach. If I couldn't figure it out, mother always told me to read the directions! Oh how I wished I had a set of directions for this Friday night!

What had I gotten myself into? I didn't know why I was worried, because I felt very comfortable around her. This time though, she would be inside my house, not inside her office! Was I really ready for this...cooking for her and then what? Here I go again, getting myself all worked up over nothing! I need to call Jackie... Oh God, I can't even remember her phone number. What is the matter with me? Looking around for my address book I could feel myself getting really tense. This is stupid...there is no reason for me to get like this. I found the book and then the number. Dialing it, I had to try to forget about this being a big deal. It was just dinner, I kept telling myself.

"Hello?"

"Jackie, hi it's me."

"Why are you so stressed Terri?"

"You can tell, huh?"

"Of course I can tell...what's up?"

"First, let me tell you that I'm twelve weeks pregnant!"

"Pregnant? Does mom know?"

"Yes, she knows and she has given me her blessing! Can you believe it? Oh, and I also have a date this Friday night...I'm cooking dinner for her."

"Who's the date with? Anyone I know?"

"As a matter of fact, you do. It's Dr. Shannon...uh, excuse me, Aubrey."

"Aubrey, is it now? How did this happen?"

"Well, she asked me to dinner about four or five weeks ago and we went to Outback. While we were there, we talked about her ex and I talked about Annie...it was really a great conversation. Anyway, we were there so late that a snowstorm kicked in and she had to take me home. One thing led to another and then she hugged me...then she kissed me!"

"You're kidding? Really?"

"Honest! It was just a soft peck...that's all."

"Well, is she something you might want to pursue?"

"I think so...I really enjoy being with her. She's a good hugger! Made me feel safe, you know? I mean, I was shocked I guess that she even did it, but I am curious about her. I want to know more."

"That's a good thing squister. Isn't it? I mean, you have been through so much coming home from being in a ten year relationship...this must be all new to you again in some ways."

"Yep, it is. Scares me to death! I don't know which end is up! To begin with, I'm having a memory lapse because of this pregnancy and I'm more tense than usual! I need to be more calm not more stressed!" Maybe this isn't good timing?"

"Listen Terri, this is perfect timing for you. To begin with, you have met someone who is really wonderful and obviously thinks the world of you...otherwise, she wouldn't want to pursue it. Second of all, this could be the closure you need to get over Annie. I know your heart is still with her, but you need to let her go and move on with your life..."

"Jackie, I know you're right about all of this...I can feel it. But, I guess it's just going to take some time getting over her. I really loved her and I guess I still do."

"Of course you do. You just can't put ten years out of your head, let alone the love you feel for her. I think Aubrey understands that, don't you?"

"I think she does in a way...I could tell somewhat from our conversations at the restaurant. I think she could see my pain. She told me that I was the better one from having loved and lost. I think she meant I was the better person, not Annie. I got so emotional over that comment that I cried, and that's when she hugged me. She apologized for saying it and then she kissed me. God, what a night."

"You sound down Terri..."

"No, not really. I'm just...I don't know. I guess I'm worried and confused about how Friday might go and what, if any, expectations she may have. I know I shouldn't worry about that stuff, but I certainly don't want to do anything that I'm not ready for, you know?"

"Terri, she knows where you stand. I promise, you don't have anything to worry about! Trust me! Look, she may not be ready either. Did you ever stop to think about that? She might be just as nervous, if not more so. I bet you will have a wonderful time Friday evening with her."

"God, I hope you're right. I'm too old for..."

"Don't even say it! You were going to say that you're too old weren't you?"

"You know me too well Jackie. It's just that I never thought about starting over when I was in my relationship with Annie. I thought we would be together forever, you know? Now, here I am almost forty, starting over again and it feels weird."

"Sounds like she's starting over too? She might think this whole concept is out of character for her as well. Since her situation was a little different from yours, she may be more ready to start over. I only say that because she was probably ready to be out of the abusive relationship. But again, don't worry. She may have some walls up too."

"You might be right about that. I never looked at it like that before."

"Listen Terri, there's something I learned a long time ago about relationships... the most important things we can learn about a person doesn't take much time. Do you understand that? All you have to do is be honest and genuine with her and cook her dinner. That's all you have to do is just be yourself. Right?"

"Right. And, I have been honest with her up to this point. I just have to figure out now what I'm going to fix her for dinner. She gave me quite a few good ideas as to the foods she likes, so it shouldn't be that difficult."

"Feel better now?"

"Actually, I do. Thank you very much. I'm not sure I would know what to do without you right now! How did you get so smart?"

"Trial and error Terri...trial and error. So, when is the baby due?"

"Well, my due date is around June 26th. But, the wild thing is that I have a possibility of having twins! We won't know any more for a few more weeks. The sonogram didn't detect anything right now."

"Twins?"

"Yes, I know...can you believe it?"

"Terri, no I can't...but more than anything...I can't believe mom gave you her blessing! Does dad know anything yet?"

"Not as far as I know...mom said she would handle both him and Gloria."

"Listen, I've got to run. If you need anything, call me! Regardless, day or night. I'm here for you."

"All right sweetie, I'll let you go. I'll call you as soon as I hear something. Bye."

"Bye Terri."

~

When I got up the next morning, I glanced outside to check the weather. Needless to say, it was cold, but not snowing as it had been the past few weeks. I'm not much for cold weather, but I knew spring would be here before I knew it. I was ready for it now.

My skin, usually dry and itchy this time of year, had taken on a whole new look. Even my hair and nails didn't seem to be so brittle. This pregnancy was doing me a lot of good these days. I felt healthier, looked healthier and had a better mental attitude. It's amazing what additional hormones can do for you. But because I was off work today, It would give me some much-needed time for me. Knowing that Friday was a few days away helped let me relax a little. I didn't feel so stressed for time or other worries. For now, I was fine. I wanted to take the time and read some of the literature Aubrey, had given me. I thought how strange it would be to call her by her first name now. I had always seen her in a professional way, so this was different to me. But, if that's what she wanted, I would agree to it. What an awesome name. I wondered what it meant.

I nestled back into bed and pulled the covers up to my neck. I grabbed the literature off the nightstand and began to read when I heard a loud splash outside. What an odd noise. If that was a fish, I would hate to see how big it was! Running to the window, I peeked out to see nothing but rings in the water. I could tell something was different. I couldn't see it yet, but I wanted to keep my eyes wide open. Grabbing the binoculars, I headed for the window again. Focusing in on the water, I started watching slowly from left to right. It was barely daylight, but I could see enough from the water's movement that something was in there. I had always heard stories about muskrats and such that lived along the banks of the lake. But I had never seen one out here. Hell, I'd never seen a hawk out here either until this year. It's no telling what's down there. Still watching through the binoculars, I kept searching the water for something to appear. It wasn't long before the rings started again on the surface of the water...the rings became continuous now and I could definitely see movement underneath. What was it? The movement stopped and now I was more curious. Staring down toward the dock, I noticed a small gap in the decking where age and weather had taken its toll. Almost instantly, I saw a sleek, black thing crawl out from under the dock and through the gap in the deck and it sat on top of the dock. I was afraid to move. Through the binoculars, I could see it resembled a seal-like animal. As I kept watching it, it began to move about the dock as if it were playing with something. It was a fish. He had caught a fish! That's what all the movement was in the water. He was actually catching fish and coming up, topside to eat them. Curious, I continued to watch him. After eating the fish, he would slither back in to try and catch more. Each time, he would crawl back up through the same gap in the decking and sit topside to eat his catch. What a remarkable animal. I wondered why I hadn't seen him before out here. I wondered what it actually was...it couldn't be a seal. They only existed in salt water. Searching through my book of animals, I looked up seal...and to my surprise, it actually had a picture of this animal on the page. Except it wasn't a seal at all, it was an otter. A river otter, to be exact. It says that we can learn from the otter to be playful, nurturing, curious, and humanitarian in nature. I wondered if this was another sign. If it was a sign, what better time than the present...

~

Friday had finally come. This could be the first day I might feel a connection...if I just let myself. I wondered if I would be able to do it. Could I let the walls come down far enough to feel another connection with anyone? If it would be with anyone, it could be with her. I trusted her and in some aspects, I could feel she might be special. But, I would have to let my walls come down and be vulnerable once again to find out. That meant I would be putting myself in a situation where all hell could break loose. Sitting out there on that limb alone...waiting. Maybe she was waiting too. Maybe Jackie was right about that. Maybe we were both sitting out there on that limb together...just waiting.

Tonight would prove to be interesting. She had already been here twice, but I had not been to her house. I wondered if she would ever ask me. I wondered what we had in common, besides this pregnancy. We apparently liked the same foods so, It would be easy for me to cook for her tonight. That's one thing I could do very well. I could cook just about anything. Even on the grill I could cook all kinds of meats and vegetables. I liked the taste of foods prepared on a grill. There was just something about cooking it outdoors that made it even better. I knew it would probably get cold tonight, but I had planned to build a fire in the fireplace. Most everyone seemed to like a fire when it was cold. I hoped that would make her feel more comfortable here. Maybe it would be a comfort zone for both of us.

What was it about women that scared me to death... maybe I was just scared of the relationship and whether or not it would last. Especially now with this pregnancy. Who would want me in this condition? Two months pregnant! Not many women I knew wanted a family...or a baby. All the women I met just wanted sex for the night...only one-night stands seem to be the thing. I wasn't up for that. I need to be in a relationship...I don't need to be, I just want to be. But, only if it will last. I don't want a fling or a one-night stand. Maybe I was just afraid to take a chance....I hated taking risks. But, I knew I had to take this risk. If I didn't, I was afraid I would regret it.

Aubrey was different. I knew I would have to compromise to have her. Someone once told me that compromising is how you negotiate yourself with others. It couldn't be more true. Aubrey would be worth any compromise or negotiation. She seemed to be so caring and understanding that last night we shared our thoughts at the restaurant. Listening to me so attentively and allowing me the time to discuss Annie and how I felt. That's how I felt being her patient, too. She just had that special touch about her that made me feel comfortable. I found her very attractive as well. I normally looked for someone with blonde hair, blue eyes and about five foot, four inches tall. Not this time. Dark brown hair, brown eyes, and about five foot, eight inches. What a contradiction of interest! Not only was she gorgeous, but smart and professional. I admired that in women. I also admire women who could live alone and have self-esteem. Most women I had known or been involved with were professional and gorgeous. I wouldn't have it any other way...or settle for anything less. Aubrey was all of that. I wondered what she felt for me, for her to be interested.

Was it the pregnancy itself? Was it my quiet nature and caring manner? Maybe she wanted a family, too. I wondered if I could ask her...what connection did she find between us. Why did she want to pursue this? I had to ask tonight. If I knew tonight, it might give me an answer whether or not to continue sitting out on that limb...

V.A. Buck

Chapter 15

Setting the table, I decided to use my best china, which depicted "The Hunt", by Noritake. I had two, five-piece place settings and wanted everything to be set perfectly at the table. I made sure the white, linen mats were pressed and the napkins were placed just so in the middle of each plate. Silverware was carefully placed to the sides of each plate. I wanted everything to flow together, from the china to the food. I decided to use crystal goblets for my specially brewed, sweet ice tea. I placed two, white candles in the center of the table and lit the candles. I hoped she would be both comfortable and impressed.

They say you only have one chance to make a good, first impression. I felt this would to be my chance to win her over. Everything had to be *flawless*. I had dusted, vacuumed, and cleaned everything from top to bottom. I didn't want her to think I was a slob...although I could be messy sometimes. I guess once the baby came, there would be plenty of messes. But tonight, no messes.

I looked through my CD's and picked out several I thought would be appropriate for during dinner and then afterwards. I hoped she liked my choices. If she didn't, I had more for her to choose from. I wanted her to feel comfortable and relaxed. The table had been set and music chosen. All I had to do now was cook dinner. I had plenty of time. Besides, it was now five o'clock and time for me to start getting ready.

I couldn't decide what I would wear. My choices were really pretty slim. Nothing was fitting right anymore. Everything was too tight, even my shirts. My breasts felt like they had doubled in size and were hard as bricks! I didn't expect that from this pregnancy. Time would tell what else would change in my body. I searched through my closets for a pair of pants that would be a pair of sweats in disguise. I didn't want to look sloppy though. I finally found a pair of khaki's and a button-down oxford shirt that fit perfectly. Thank God I didn't have to wear a pair of sweats for a night like tonight! I would rather cancel the date than come to dinner dressed like that! I wanted to make a great impression on her, not repulse her. I'll definitely have to go maternity clothes shopping this weekend. I can't keep struggling to find clothes in this closet I know won't fit! Maybe she would want to go shopping with me? That's a great topic of conversation...shopping! Every woman I know loves to shop. Pulling out the ironing board, I found the spray starch. There's nothing like a starched button-down, oxford shirt and a crisp pair of khakis to look and feel preppy. I was far from being preppy, but I admired the clean-cut look. I didn't mind ironing as long as it gave me the look I felt comfortable with.

I had just come out of the bedroom when I heard the phone ring. Oh God, I hope she's not canceling...

"Hello?"

"Hello dear, how are you feeling tonight?"

"Hi Mom. Is everything all right?"

"Yes, of course. Listen, the reason I'm calling you is to tell you we're dropping by tonight to bring you some things for the baby. I told your father and at first, he didn't take things so well. But, today he's like a different man! He is so excited about you having a child! All he keeps talking about is the fact he is going to be a grandfather! So, will you be home tonight?"

"I'm glad he is excited. Actually mom, I'm having company tonight. What about tomorrow afternoon? Would that be okay?"

"Oh, that will be fine. I'll tell your father and we'll see you tomorrow afternoon, okay? We love you dear! Bye."

"I love you too, mom and I'll see you both tomorrow. Bye."

Whew, what a relief... I could just see both of them stopping by, unannounced and catch a glimpse of who I was having dinner with. They knew I was a lesbian, but it was never discussed openly. Sometimes, things are better left unsaid where they're concerned. Other times, I wished I could tell them everything. I was in a no-win situation, most of the time with them. I knew what they were probably thinking, but I didn't care. I was a grown woman and could live my life the way I wanted. I was living it, not them.

I looked around the house to make sure everything looked clean. The fire was built and I was ready to start the grill. It wouldn't take very long to cook the dinner. The salad was ready. The chicken had been marinating for several hours. The potatoes would be ready by seven and the tea was chilling in the fridge. All I had to do was cook the chicken.

I heard what I thought was a car pulling up the driveway. She must be here. The doorbell rang. I walked to the front door, opened it to find Aubrey standing there holding a bottle of wine. She was smiling, as usual, offered me the bottle of wine and I invited her in. I took her long, navy dress coat and laid it in on the bed and when I returned, she was standing in front of the fireplace, warming her hands. I noticed she had painted her nails a soft burgundy color that emphasized her dark skin. She looked beautiful. She had her hair pulled back in a braid that rested against the back of her red, turtleneck sweater. Her gold, hoop earrings glistened as they swayed back and forth with the slightest tilt of her head. She had on a pair of khakis too that were neatly pressed with a pair of tasseled, cordovan loafers. She looked sexy, yet sharp, dressed that way. You would never know she was a doctor, unless you saw her wearing a lab coat. For some reason, she just didn't have the typical doctor look. She was different in that aspect. I didn't care at this point, I was just glad she was here. I opened the bottle of wine, offered her a glass, and then returned to kitchen to get dinner underway.

I wondered if I could get use to that portrait. Her, standing there by the fireplace, drinking a glass of wine. Wow, what a pleasingly, picturesque woman. I couldn't take my eyes off her. Without a doubt, I was attracted to her. I couldn't help but stare...she was beautiful. She could just about take my breath away if I let her. I felt almost as if I was in my own little fantasy world. Actually, I liked being there at the moment, just to see how much longer I could get away with staring at her before she caught on to me. I hadn't felt this way in such a long time, but I liked the feeling. If I let myself, I know I could probably fall in-love with her. Jackie was right...she was everything I had been searching for. Not only was she beautiful on the outside, but she was also tender and caring on the inside. I could tell she had a big heart, and I could get use to that in a hurry. Women like Aubrey were hard to come by these days. I felt blessed to have her in my life now. I wasn't sure where she and I were going, but I believe I was ready to sit out on that limb a little longer and run the risks to find out. This little fantasy I was in at the moment was beginning to come to a screeching halt when I saw her look toward my way. I certainly didn't want her to think I had been staring at her this entire time, so I finally pulled myself together quickly.

"Are you getting hungry yet, Aubrey?"

I have to admit, it's going to take me a little while getting use to calling her by her first name. She has been my doctor for such a long time now, that it feels a little awkward.

"I am starving! I was so busy today that I didn't have time to eat lunch! We were swamped!"

"No problem, I am putting the chicken on the grill as we speak! It will be done in just a little while. In the meantime, I'll put on some music. Is that okay with you?"

"Sure."

"If you don't like this, I have other music you can choose from in my CD case."

"Oh, I'm sure it will be fine. I'm not too picky. I like just about everything."

"What do you listen to when you're not at the office?"

"I listen to Jazz, Folk, Alternative music styles. It's usually what's playing in my office and clinic. Did you hear it while you were in the waiting room?"

"Yes, I did. I thought it was so relaxing. It almost put me to sleep once, while I waited. I have music by classical artists and alternative musicians, too. George Winston, Yanni, and others. Do you listen to any of them?"

"All the time!"

"Hold on, I'll be right back, let me go check on the grill."

After turning the chicken, I peeked in through the window and saw her sitting on the couch, nonchalantly. I just wanted to stare...what a sight. We seem to have some things in common...more than I thought we would. I had to get back in there. I didn't want to be rude. Besides, I wanted a closer look!

"Do you need any help with...cooking or anything?"

"No, I want you to sit, relax and drink your glass of wine. Sounds as though you've had quite a day. Is it always that busy on a Friday or did your secretary overbook your schedule?"

"Actually, I can't remember when it's been this busy. She may have over-booked a bit. But, enough about my day and me. Tell me how you're feeling with the pregnancy?"

"Physically or mentally?"

"Both."

"Wow, I am just trying to absorb it all. Sometimes, I feel pressed for time...like I don't have enough time to get everything ready for the baby, you know? I don't even have a room set up yet...no baby things...although, mom did call earlier and said they were going to come over to bring some stuff. I need to go shopping actually for some maternity clothes. Would you like to go with me sometime?"

"I would love to go! Just let me know when. I know I great little store that deals in second-hand maternity things, but in great shape. Do you remember where you turn to come into my clinic...right there on the corner before you turn is a side street called Backstreet Avenue. Do you know where I'm talking about?"

"Yes, I remember it now. That sounds great, we'll have to go there!"

"I send all my patients there. She always appreciates the business."

"Good, we'll go there first! When can you go?"

"I can go one day after work or whenever is a convenient time for you. You just let me know when you're ready."

"Hold that thought and let me check the chicken."

The chicken was ready and I brought everything out from the fridge and sat it on the counter. I tossed the salad one more time, placed several salad dressings on the table, put ice in the glasses, poured the tea, and took the potatoes out of the oven. Everything was ready.

"Are you ready? I hope you're hungry because we have a huge meal to consume!"

"I am starving!"

I invited her to come into the dining room to eat. She pulled out her chair, sat and placed her napkin in her lap. I began by passing the food to her first. After she served herself, I then served myself and sat across from her. She waited for me to sit before starting to eat. How considerate, I thought.

"Do you need more wine, or is tea okay for dinner?"

"No, the tea is fine. I'll wait until after dinner for another glass. Did you get a glass of wine?"

"No, I promise, I didn't. I would be too worried about the baby! I'm already worried about all the changes my body will go through between now and the delivery. Actually, I can already feel some changes that are occurring and wonder if it's normal to be feeling this way."

"Tell me what you've noticed so far. Have you had any morning sickness yet?"

"No, thank God! My belly is getting bigger. My chest is sore, very hard, and feel as though they have doubled in size! Is that normal?"

"Yes, it is. Tell me what else you've noticed."

"So far, that's all. Is there anything else that I should be noticing? Oh. Wait, I did notice something else, but I haven't felt it since I was your at office last. I felt a pull when I got out of the car. Is that anything to be concerned about?"

"You say it hasn't occurred since then?"

"No, not that I can recall."

"If it does happen again, it might just be an odd way you're moving. Keep tabs on when it does occur, okay?"

"I will. By the way, is there anything I can get you or anything you need?"

"No, everything is wonderful. I'm fine for now."

I watched her for a moment and could tell something was on her mind. She had that look on her face like she was distracted by something. I wondered if the dinner was okay or if something else was bothering her. She looked up, caught me staring at her and I quickly looked away.

"Listen, I wanted to continue our conversation from the restaurant. If that's okay with you?"

"Of course…what would you like to talk about?"

I took a deep breath and let it out very slowly.

"Don't worry, it's nothing to worry about. I just wanted to pursue some other avenues from our conversations, that's all."

"Other avenues?"

"It's just that… It's about the connection between you and me. We seem to have a connection about a lot of things. For one, this pregnancy. Being your doctor, I want to help you in whatever way I can. I too, have wanted a child for a long time, but I had a hysterectomy a couple of years ago. Somehow, I feel as though I am living this pregnancy through you. I don't know how else to describe it. When I first saw you in the clinic and you told me what you wanted to accomplish, I too had done the same. Unfortunately, I wasn't physically able to pursue it. My doctor told me I wouldn't be able to have children. You, on the other hand, are very fortunate you were able to get pregnant. Don't get me wrong, I'm very happy for you and I want this to be the most incredible experience you've ever had."

"What exactly are you trying to say...that you want to be a part of my pregnancy? I'm not sure I fully understand. You are a part of my life as my doctor and will remain so even when I deliver this baby. I need you to be there for me every step of the way, Aubrey."

"I guess what I'm trying to say is that I do want to be there every step of the way...I want to help you experience this to the fullest."

"Why wouldn't you? You're my doctor... Unless you don't want to be anymore? Is that what you're trying to say?"

"No, of course not! How can I put this..."

What in the hell was she trying to tell me? I was so confused with this conversation that she had me worried at this point. She obviously felt uncomfortable about something.

"Just spit it out Aubrey...you're about to make me worry...What are you feeling so uncomfortable about? Did I say something wrong?"

I took a big swallow of my tea and at that moment, wished it had been wine! I was really starting to be concerned. I could tell something was different about her tonight. She seemed consumed by something. I wondered if I had inadvertently said something that could have triggered negative feelings about Katie.

"No, you haven't said anything wrong. That's just it Terri, you never say anything wrong. It's always something positive or caring when you do say something to me. Katie was always negative and hurtful. That's the difference between you two...actually there's a great deal that's different between you both. I've never known someone like you that's...well, someone that's everything I've wanted to be. Does that make any sense? I guess what I'm trying to tell you is that you are a mentor to me and I want to continue to be a part of your life...even if it's just as your doctor."

"A mentor? You consider me a mentor to you? Wow, I'm flattered... You have no idea how much I need you right now, do you? Not only as my doctor, Aubrey, but also as my friend. I have never been through this before and I am scared to death! You will have to be my ears, eyes, and mind throughout this pregnancy. Because, quite frankly, I don't have a clue. Do you know how much I am depending on you? I don't think you do, Aubrey. You are the most knowledgeable woman I know. First of all, I checked you out thoroughly before I even came to you. I did that because I wanted the best doctor possible. Everyone I asked said you were the best. Yes, the best. If you weren't, you wouldn't be my doctor right now. I promise you that much. I value your opinions, knowledge, experience, and friendship. Without any of those things, I wouldn't be where I am right now. I wouldn't be pregnant or having a wonderful dinner with you. You are obviously in my life for a reason... For whatever reason, I don't want you going anywhere. I want you to remain where you are right now, because I can't do this alone. Yes, I have my family and friends, but I need you to be there for me. I feel comfortable with you. You make me feel right about this pregnancy. There is a connection here...and right now, that's all I can acknowledge. That's all I can see or feel...is that connection...to you. Does that scare you that I feel a connection to you, too?"

"Now I'm flattered. I had no idea you felt that way about me as your doctor or as a friend. I don't quite know what to say. No one has ever said that to me before. Just to know that is a good feeling. I can't imagine that I would find someone like you to be so caring or honest with their feelings. Katie was never like that with me....never."

We finished our dinner and she helped me clear the table. We stacked all the dishes on the counter and then made our way into the living room to continue our conversations. The music was still playing and the fire was almost out. I placed more wood in the fireplace and it started back up in a roaring blaze. I could tell it was getting colder outside from the condensation on the inside of the windows. I stepped outside to grab a few more pieces of wood when I noticed it had started to snow again. How ironic....every time she is here, it snows. It never fails. It had to be fate. Meeting her was fate, I thought. I wondered what was going through her mind. How ironic too that she thought of me as a mentor. Her relationship with Katie must have been hell.

Coming in from outside, I poured myself another glass of tea and asked if she was ready for another glass of wine. She nodded and as I walked over and filled her glass, I could sense she was ready to resume the conversations... I could feel it was going to get deep.

I sat across from her in my recliner so I could see her, in all my amazement, how beautiful she was to me. She didn't have to do a thing, but sit there. I was glad she would let me have dinner with her. I needed it, I thought, to get to know her tonight. Being so attracted to her was catching me off guard. I never thought I could be attracted to someone, so quickly, since I had returned home. I was very drawn to her....not just her beauty, but her whole being. I liked what she was about. She had no idea I felt this way about her and I certainly wasn't going to tell her tonight. I'll just sit here and be patient and wait for her to continue. I was ready for just about anything she was about to say. Drinking her second glass of wine, she looked up at me. Her eyes looked like they were dancing, but it was only the reflection from fire.

"Tell me something, Terri....how did you get to this point in your life, where you made the decision to have a baby? You obviously wanted one earlier in life, when you were in Ohio, but you chose to wait... Why did you wait?"

"It just didn't feel right at the time Aubrey. I guess a part of me, deep down, knew that the relationship was in trouble and I didn't like the idea of leaving a baby behind. I couldn't have handled it. It was hard enough leaving her. It feels right now because I have almost everything in my life I could possibly want...you know, like material things. I'm ready to share my life unconditionally now. Does that make sense? It's like there's something missing in my life, in a way. I'm missing a partner in my life to share this wonderful experience with, too. I'm glad, in a way, I didn't have a baby with Annie. It didn't feel right in the spiritual sense, either. Besides, she wasn't a big believer in God. She had to see something before she could believe in it...and I'm not like that. I guess what I'm trying to say is that I have faith. She was always searching for something. She always told me that a child would make her feel complete. But, I didn't believe that. I believed she was missing her spirituality. I don't think she was an Atheist exactly, I just don't think she knew what to believe at times."

"Katie and I talked about having a child together, but like you, I felt the relationship was going nowhere and in trouble. I didn't feel good about the idea of raising a child with an alcoholic mother. I didn't want to put the child through that. Besides, it was always in the back of my mind that the child could have been taken away from me because of the laws about lesbian mothers. Now, I wouldn't think twice about it...I would have a child today if I could and if I met the right person to share the experience with. Whenever you come into my office, I can't help but wonder what my life would be like now if I were going through the same as you. I guess in a way, I am somewhat envious of your pregnancy. You had the guts to go through with it. Maybe that's the connection I have with you. Well, at least part of the connection I feel when I am around you."

"What do you mean by part of the connection you feel for me?"

"I was hoping you wouldn't ask me that... I'm not sure you're ready to hear what I have to say about...how I really feel about you."

"Aubrey, what ever it is, I'm sure I can handle it. I'm big girl, you know. Besides, if I can handle being pregnant, I can handle just about anything! Tell me what's on your mind."

I was enjoying this conversation with her. But I could tell whatever she was about to say wasn't going to be easy. It just didn't matter to me anymore. I knew I could handle it. I almost hoped she would say that she was falling in-love with me. What I felt for her, I wasn't sure. But I knew I could have a relationship with her...she could help me forget and help me heal. I was sure of that. It seemed I could do the same for her...I could tell she was hurting. She had been through a lot with Katie.

"Let me first tell you that I loved Katie. I don't think I was ever in-love with her, but I loved her. Because of how she hurt me and our relationship, I didn't want to trust again. Then I met you. You are so different from her that it makes it so easy for me to trust. It scares me how much I do trust you. As your doctor, you trust me and I realize that, but I want you to be able to trust me outside of that professional relationship. Can you do that? I mean, can you trust me outside the clinic and inside your personal life?"

"Aubrey, if I didn't think I could trust you, you wouldn't be here, in my house, having dinner with me. Of course I trust you... How can I convince you of that? Listen, I loved Annie, too. Not only was I in-love with her, but also I trusted her with my life. Yes, our situations were different, but my trust factor was just as damaged. Let me tell you this. When I see you sitting there, on my couch, I simply can't believe you are here. Sometimes, I think to myself that I'm unworthy of your presence. Look at you! You are absolutely stunning. But it's not only your beauty that I find attractive, it's all of you. It's also about the connection that you and I have. I don't know where it came from or why, but it's here. You're here and that's all that matters. Yes, I trust you. You make it easy for me to trust you because of who you are...a very caring doctor and person. Does that answer your question?"

"Yes, I think so. It sounded like you just told me you are attracted to me. Did I misunderstand what you said?"

Oh my God, I have done what I said I wouldn't do! I told myself I wouldn't tell her tonight and it just came flying out before I could stop it! Well, I have to tell her the truth...damn it.

"No...you didn't misunderstand. I think you are extremely attractive. So much so, that's it's all I can do...not to stare. I hope you don't find that juvenile. Actually, I'm having a hard time admitting to the fact that I am attracted to you. Please don't take that the wrong way. It's just that I never thought I would find someone else attractive, this soon, since I moved home. I wasn't looking for another woman. All I can tell you at this point is that I find you incredibly attractive. Does that scare you?"

I saw her start to smile as her eyes focused in on mine. She tilted her head slightly, as if she were listening very closely to what I said. Her gold, hoop earrings bounced slightly off her cheek and then fell back into place as she started to answer my question.

"No, that doesn't scare me and neither do you. If you did, I wouldn't have kissed you before. Remember? Besides, I wanted to take you home and kiss you. I'm just sorry that I made you cry."

"Aubrey, you didn't make me cry...remembering the hurt did. Yes, I was shocked that you kissed me, but only because it was so soon...and you hardly know me. I still feel the hurt, as I'm sure you've figured out by now. But, in time I'll forget. You can help me do that."

There, I had said it. We continued to talk for hours about this and that and when she finally finished the bottle of wine, I was exhausted. Time had finally caught up with me. It was nearly three in the morning and she was still here. When I went to look out the window, I saw the snow was still coming down. We had more than our share of accumulation. There must have been at least six inches of snow by now. The drifts were more than that. I wondered if I should ask her to stay or if she would feel comfortable enough to do that. After watching it snow more by the minute, I turned and she was putting on her coat and gloves. She was getting ready to leave.

"Are you going to be okay driving home? I mean with the wine and the weather?"

"Of course I will be fine. I have to go in to work for half a day tomorrow...rather, today. So, I need to get going so that I can get some rest before work. I'll be fine, I promise."

"You're welcome to stay here if you like and get some rest."

"I appreciate the offer, but I really must go. Maybe another time?"

"I'll hold you to it!"

"Thank you so much for a wonderful dinner and conversation. I really had a great time. I've learned so much about you these past few hours...and by the way, that's a good thing."

"I'm glad you enjoyed the dinner and our talks. We'll have to do it again soon."

I gave her a hug, opened the door and away she went out into the early, snowy morning. I was worried about her driving in this mess, but she did have a 4-wheel drive. Watching her slowly drive away, I thought for a minute about our first date. I went back in, closed and locked the door and headed for my pajamas. I was so tired; I could hardly keep my eyes open or put one foot in front of the other. I fell into bed and what seemed like seconds, I was asleep.

Chapter 16

As I started cleaning up from last night's dinner, I realized today would be a whole different day. I thought about last night's conversations, and felt more confident that I could be in a relationship with her. But, I wanted to go slow...I wanted to learn more about her and about Katie. I had a feeling she wasn't telling me everything. I could tell she wasn't ready to divulge all the bits and pieces of their haunting past. But, when she was ready, I know she could trust me enough to tell me. I was glad I was honest with her last night. I could have told her so much more, but it seemed she wanted to reveal more about herself than me. I knew I would be seeing her more frequently now that the baby was growing. I hoped I would be able to see her outside of her office as well. My visits to her clinic will give me a chance to at least see her...even if the visits would be short. I didn't care. I was at the point now where I wanted to see her more anyway. I didn't care how or where...I just wanted to see her.

My next appointment with her wasn't until next month. Hopefully, I will be able to learn more about the baby when she does another sonogram. I was starting my third month, and now was the time to start shopping for some maternity clothes. I couldn't believe how much my belly had developed into a cantaloupe! I felt so swollen and bloated. I knew it was only going to get worse from here on. I hoped she would go with me to that little place near her office. Maybe she could go with me to other places as well because I needed lots of things for the baby.

I wondered what mom and dad would bring over this afternoon. Hopefully, they would bring some things I could really use. Maybe they will bring the baby a crib too! I would have to get my other bedroom ready for the baby soon and maybe mother could help me with that as well. If she couldn't, maybe Aubrey could. I was eager for them to arrive today so that I could get started on my list for what I needed later on. Whatever I needed, I could always ask for my baby shower. Maybe I needed to get registered somewhere?

Timing was everything now. It was getting closer and closer to the due date. It seemed not too long ago when I just went in for the procedure and now I'm already in my third month. Before I know it, it will be time to deliver. I had to make every day count. I felt like I was running out of time. Mother and dad were scheduled to arrive any minute and I finally finished cleaning up last night's dishes. Thank God for disposals, dishwashers, and compactors! I don't know what I'd do without them. I'm quite sure they'll all come in handy when the baby arrives.

The doorbell rang and when I opened the door, I found mother and dad standing on the front porch with several, large packages in their hands.

"Hi guys, what in the world do you have in all those bags?"

"Well, your father and I have been going through the leftover baby stuff from all of you girls and we thought you would be able to use it! I can't wait to show you what we came up with!"

"That's wonderful mom! Come in so you can show me! How are you doing dad, with all of this baby news?"

"Needless to say, when I first found out...I was shocked. Now, I am excited I'm going to be a grandfather...I would have never believed it if you're mother hadn't told me herself."

"What can't you believe...that you're going to be a grandfather or me, being pregnant?"

"I guess both! I just assumed that Jackie would be the one to give us a grandchild, not you."

"Well dad, wonders never cease, do they? Anyway, I'm glad you're excited about being a grandfather! You'll be a great one, too."

"Thanks honey. You'll be a terrific mother." While I gave him a hug, I smiled at mom.

We all started ripping open the bags and then laughed. It seemed like Christmas...only it was November, not December. She started reminiscing about one piece or another and then she came to a book. I saw tears come to her eyes as she opened it and looked at the pictures.

"I started reading this book to you before you were even born. I would sit in the baby room, rock in the rocking chair and read aloud. Somehow, I knew you heard every word. They say that babies can hear what you're saying, even before they're born. Now, you can do the same with your child."

She handed me the book and I made a silent promise to myself that I would do exactly that. How wonderful it would be to read to my child before he was born. I couldn't believe how sentimental she was with all of our baby things. I imagined I would be the same way. I probably wouldn't give up anything of my child's things. I was beginning to understand this maternal bond between mother and child. Mother continued to go through each bag of clothes and describe an exact situation when one of us had worn it. How amazing this was to me that she could recall exact days and what we were doing when we wore them. Even a small stain on a shirt brought about a story. I hope my memory would be as good as hers, when it came time for me to do the same with my son. This must be an incredible joyous time for her to share all this with me. I wished Jackie were here with us going through all this baby stuff. She would get a kick out of it. I hoped she wouldn't mind me using some of her baby stuff for my son. Even Gloria's stuff was here as well. I'm sure she wouldn't mind...at least I hoped not.

"Listen mom, did you get a chance to speak to Gloria about using some of her baby stuff? I mean, do you think she would mind me using it?"

"I did talk to her about it first and she was fine with it. She actually wanted to come with us today, but she had already made plans to do something else. She's....she's excited for you dear."

"Excited for me? You've got to be kidding!"

"No, seriously...she's very excited for you....and Jackie is too!"

My whole family was giving me support, I had a wonderful doctor and new friend, and I was pregnant. Everything had fallen into place. Both balance and harmony had come my way... what else could I possibly want or need? There were so many pieces of clothing, aging from infant to toddler. I hoped I would be able to use most, if not all of it. There were even toys in the packages they brought. Some of them even I recognized. I was glad mom had saved all of our things, because I surely couldn't afford to go out and buy all new things. We finished going through everything they brought and mother stood up and said, "there was one more thing we brought, but your dad will have to bring it in."

What in the world could they have brought now? I sat still while he walked out the front door. Dad was struggling to open the door with something in both hands, when mom rushed to the door to help him. I stood back and waited. Just as mom opened the door for him, in walked dad with the most beautiful wooden baby crib I had ever seen. He brought it into the living room and set it down gently. Being emotional as I was already, I looked at both of them and started to cry. Mom came over and hugged me while I cried and dad was saying something to the effect that the crib wasn't that big of deal. I think I cried harder at that moment. He didn't understand why I was crying. I never thought they would understand, let alone be this generous.

~

Going back to see Aubrey for my check up was something I looked forward to. I hadn't seen or heard from her in a few weeks. Well, I hadn't called her either. Sometimes, I don't think I see her as often as I would like. But, I would see her today and she could give me more insight about the baby. I wanted to tell her about all the baby things my parents had brought over and for some reason, I wanted to show them to her, too. I wanted her to be as involved as possible...in this pregnancy and after the baby was born. I wanted her to be involved in my life...I'm not sure how she would feel about that, but I wanted to tell her today at my appointment.

Truthfully, I'm not really sure how involved I want her to be in my life after the baby is born. I just know I want her in my life. I have a feeling she wants to be involved too, but doesn't want to overstep that family boundary line. You know, the one where your parents feel they know best about everything and everyone else is just on stand-by mode? Don't get me wrong, I'm glad my family wants to be involved. I never thought they would be. But when it came to Aubrey, not only would she be my doctor, but she would also be involved in my life. Some how, some way. My parents should be happy that I have such a wonderful friend. Somehow, I'll have to introduce her *into* the family. Maybe then, they would understand her position and connection to me. I know mother already liked her as a doctor, but dad didn't really know her. He would some day and I would make sure of it.

Strange as it may seem, I think if I had to make a decision today about her being in my life and helping me raise this child, I believe I would ask her. I think she wants to anyway. By our last conversation, I think she regrets not being able to have a child. That's part of our connection with each other. Maybe it's too soon to even talk about such things, but I feel so comfortable with and connected to her. God knows I'm extremely attracted to her! Who wouldn't be? I feel special that she even wants to share her time with me.

I was starting to get ready for my appointment, when I realized I really didn't know that much about her. I didn't know anything about her family. I knew she was born in Germany, raised in Queens, and moved her medical practice here from Boston. Well and I know about Katie. But, that's all I know about her and her family. Maybe when she's more comfortable with me, she'll tell me. I wondered if I became more open with her that she might do the same. Maybe by sharing all these baby things with her would help. I think she would enjoy seeing some of my baby things as well. Seeing each other today might give us answers we've both needed.

It's getting closer to the holidays and I want to invite her to our traditional dinners. She might have her own family in for the holidays though. I just don't want her to spend the holidays alone if her family can't come down to Tennessee or if she's not traveling north. I hope she stays here so that we can spend some quality time together. So many questions to ask...especially about the baby. I can't wait until I see her.

All these thoughts are flying at least one hundred miles an hour! It's as if I have too much on the brain! I have to deal with this pregnancy and a new friend... Why did I let myself go there! I knew this would put more stress in my life...but, it's a good stress in a way. Besides, I need to get over Annie. By meeting someone new, I can get over her more quickly and move on with my new life. I knew that. I knew that's what it would take for me to have the closure I needed. I definitely need her in my life...and I think she needs me, too. Maybe, we give each other the balance we need in our lives. I never thought I would meet someone again who could make me happy or feel complete.

"Good morning. I have an appointment this morning at ten."

"How are you feeling Terri? Any morning Sickness or other problems?"

"Fortunately, I have had no morning sickness! I can't think of anything out of the ordinary that is happening right now..."

"Okay, well, she will be with you in just a few minutes. Have a seat, and we'll call you when she's ready."

Once again, I sat down in the waiting room and waited. There were several mothers-to-be in the waiting room as well, waiting to see her. She looked really busy today as if she were running behind schedule. I certainly didn't mind to wait. Just getting to see her would make my day. I couldn't forget that cold night she stood in front of my fireplace, warming her hands. She was so very beautiful...

"Terri? Ready to come on back?"

My intimate thoughts of her were abruptly ended as the nurse entered the waiting room and asked if I were ready.

I nodded, walked in through the door and into an examining room. She handed me a gown, turned and closed the door behind her. After putting on the gown, I sat on the table and waited for her to come in. I picked up a pregnancy magazine off the counter and flipped through the pages. I came to an article where it discussed all nine months of pregnancy. This was exactly what I needed to read! How I'm supposed to feel, what's going on with the baby, and what to do during each month. Wow, this would really educate me about my pregnancy and what to expect next. I needed to be more educated, I thought. I wondered if there were any other mothers-to-be out there who were just as ignorant about theirs. I doubted it!

Since I was in my third month, I began reading about the fetus and what he is starting to look like. I was amazed that he would even have finger and toenails by now. He didn't weigh but a little more than an ounce! How tiny he is right now...

There was a knock on the door and then she entered. Reviewing my chart, she came over to the table and sat on her stainless steel, stool. She finally looked up and smiled when she asked, "how have you been feeling these past few weeks? Any nausea or weak stomach?"

"No, actually I haven't. My chest is still extremely sore and I feel as though they are really getting hard. It hurts to lay on them when I sleep."

"They will be sore for awhile because they are getting ready for breast milk. Do you plan on breast feeding?"

"Yes, I will. I understand that it will help the baby in the long run with his immune system and will also help me with the soreness."

She smiled happily when she said, "you have been reading the literature! I hoped it had helped you learn a little bit more about your body and what's happening during your pregnancy. I can see that it has helped."

I felt proud as ever! I picked up the magazine I had been reading when she entered the room and showed her the article about the nine months of pregnancy.

"That's a great learning tool for first-time mothers! That doesn't explain everything, but it gives you a monthly account of what to expect...kind of a play-by-play action plan. Let's go ahead and do another sonogram and see if we can detect anymore sounds or sights, okay? Just lie back and I'll place more of this gel on your belly." I could see her watching me as she squeezed the gel from the tube onto my belly. She was looking at my belly and I couldn't help but wonder what she was thinking. I kept watching her face and eyes. Finally, I had to ask.

"I have something I would like to ask you... I was...I was wondering when we could get together again? I really enjoyed your company and our topics of conversation so much the last time we got together. I also have some things for the baby I would like to show you."

"What about this Saturday afternoon? Will that be a good time for you? Maybe we could meet for lunch first and then go to the little second hand store, right around the corner, for maternity clothes and baby things? Then afterwards, you can show me what you have for the baby? Actually, I would like to have you over for dinner. How does that sound?"

"Meeting for lunch is an excellent idea! Shopping and dinner sounds good, too! My parents stopped by last Saturday afternoon with several packages. They brought things of mine when I was a baby. I might not be able to use everything, but it will be a start."

I continued to lie there while she used the sonogram machine. She kept watching the monitor, hardly looking up at all. I was getting a little nervous by watching her. She studied it very closely and each move she made with the instrument across my belly, was ever so slight. I watched her hands move inch by inch. She had small hands and they left me with the impression of being soft and smooth. I wondered how they would feel over my entire body. Her nails were short, well-kept and neatly painted. I caught myself embarrassed by my thoughts for a minute...but that soon dissipated when she turned to look at me.

"I still see only one. Looks as though no twins. Let's see if I can hear anything different."

She took her stethoscope and positioned it carefully on my belly. She placed it again at various locations and angles, waiting and listening for something different from before. I laid on the table, very still, so I wouldn't make any sounds that would interfere with what she was trying to hear. I watched her face focus on the sounds. She used a special sound-wave stethoscope, once again, so I could hear. She finally looked at me and smiled.

"Hear that? What you are hearing is *one* heartbeat. I don't hear another one. Looks as though you are having one healthy baby, not two. Are you disappointed?"

"No, I'm just happy I'm having one!"

"I know you must be very happy. By the way, did I give you prenatal vitamins the last time you were here? I can't remember and I don't see it in your chart anywhere."

"No, I didn't get any the last time. Do you have any samples I can take, because sometimes I have a hard time with the iron in them? I'd rather not get a prescription filled if I can't tolerate it."

"That's no problem, I've got plenty of samples. I'll get you started on one in particular and see how you do, okay? You'll just have to let me know if it upsets your stomach. By the way, how do you stay in such good shape? Your muscle tone, from looking at your stomach, is in great condition."

"Well, I'm not sure...I mean, I don't work out if that's what you're asking... I just try to eat right and I do quite a bit of physical labor."

"Physical labor? Does that include lifting and if so, how much?"

"Probably nothing over thirty or forty pounds. Is that a problem?"

"Well, that depends...are you straining to lift that much or does it come easy for you?"

"Sometimes, I have to strain. It depends on what it is I'm lifting."

"Whatever you're doing, don't lift more than twenty pounds, comfortably. If you do, it might complicate the pregnancy and the baby. Understand?"

"I promise, nothing more than twenty pounds. I also wanted to ask you about something else related to the pregnancy... What about my appointments during the holidays? Is your family coming in or are you going away for Thanksgiving or even Christmas?"

"I usually fly home to Boston for a week during Christmas, but it also depends on the weather. It's too long to drive and besides, if the weather is bad, I'll just stay here. Otherwise, I have a Doctor fill in while I'm gone that week."

"Oh, okay..."

"Don't worry, I'll give you a number where I can be reached in case of an emergency. I haven't bought my plane ticket yet anyway, because this weather has been so crazy this year. Any other questions?"

"I know you're very busy today, so the rest can wait until Saturday, okay?"

"That's fine Terri, I'm looking forward to it. I'll call you later for a time when we can meet on Saturday, okay?"

"Sounds great!"

"Stop by the front desk before you leave. They should have some prenatal vitamin samples ready for you. Try them and see how they work. If they're too strong, let me know and we can try something different. Also, remember your lifting quota…up to twenty pounds, and no more. You're getting ready for your second trimester and you'll feel more energy with the vitamins. It's all about stamina…start increasing your exercise and food in-take, only in moderation, though. It will help get rid of the sluggish feeling, in the long run."

Listening carefully to her directions, I assured her I would do everything she asked.

Chapter 17

Oversleeping wasn't something I did often, but today I did. I was feeling more tired than usual. After eating breakfast and taking one of my prenatal vitamins, I was ready to shop with Aubrey. More than anything, I was ready to spend some quality time with her. She was really making me feel more and more comfortable with this pregnancy and our friendship as well. I knew it wouldn't be long before our friendship would blossom into something more.

She had invited me over for dinner tonight and now I would be able to see her home for the first time. I envisioned at least a two-story, brick home surrounded by huge oak trees with a white picket fence in the front yard. She probably lived in the Laurel Woods Subdivision across town. That's where most of the doctors live, who work in the city. The wooded neighborhood was very quaint with brick streets, large homes, children running through the yards and expensive vehicles parked in each driveway. I could only imagine what the homes looked like on the inside. Probably a castle compared to mine. I would find out soon enough if she lived in that subdivision. As I attempted to visualize where she lived, I realized it didn't matter. Allowing me to visit her home would be enough for me.

I realized I had to start getting my own home in order and ready for my son. The second bedroom would be the baby's room and I had to start painting and decorating in the baby decor for him. Baby furniture was soon to follow on the list...after maternity clothes for me. Maybe I would find something today at the second-hand store while we were there today. Besides finding baby furniture, I had to get registered somewhere for my baby shower. Who was going to give me a shower? If there was anyone who would be able to give me a shower, it would be Jackie. But she was so far away.

We were so emotionally close, it wouldn't surprise me if she were feeling some of the same physical discomforts. I wished she were here to help me go through this. I missed her, especially when I needed to voice my opinions or needed simple reassurance about myself. It seemed we all needed that once in awhile. I think it's a woman thing...maybe even a sister thing. Regardless, it's reassurance I needed right now...even from Aubrey. I wanted more than any thing for her to be a part of my life...not just as my doctor but as my friend.

Yes, I needed her friendship but I also needed her in my life in other ways. I fantasized about her being beside me when I would wake up in the mornings. I thought about her truck parked outside in the driveway beside my car. I knew all of this was a fantasy...but she was all I thought about lately. I guess I must be losing my mind because I thought of such things.

God, how I've missed the companionship, partnership, balance, harmony, valued opinion...the trust. Getting up on Sunday mornings and watching a good movie from the sleeper sofa. Then, staying in our pajamas all day. And, when it was pouring down the rain, we built a fire in the fireplace and made love on the floor. I miss it all. The body, soul, and spirit connection. It was our silent way of saying how much we loved each other. I wondered if I would ever have that connection again. Just the touch of a hand, a smile, a phone call at two in the morning, a vase full of her favorite flowers, and a favorite restaurant. Just the simplest things that made me happy are still deeply implanted in a space where I don't think even she could reach. I still worry about being out on that limb alone; being able to make her happy or being able to please her. I guess I worry too much...but it's a woman thing to worry.

~

"I'll meet you at twelve noon, at Ruby Tuesday's for lunch...is that okay with you or does that give you enough time?"

"Yes, that's fine! I'm about twenty minutes out, so I'll be leaving here in a few minutes. Are you still at work?"

"Yes, I'm finishing up here with a patient and then I'll be leaving in about fifteen minutes."

Hanging up the phone, I gathered up a few things mom had brought, like the book and a few pieces of clothing for the baby. I wanted her to see them. I also wanted to ask her hypothetically, about reading to the baby before he's born. I wanted her astute, doctoral opinion on the subject. I had a feeling I already knew what she would say, but I wanted her opinion anyway.

It was suppose to be a nice day today with no snow or rain in the forecast. Finally, a nice sunny day with only a jacket to wear. It figures, since the holidays are right around the corner! With bag in hand, I was off to meet her for lunch. Pulling in the parking lot, there wasn't a parking space available for what seemed like blocks. I would have to walk from the back forty! Well, she said I needed more exercise anyway, so what better time to start than now. It was in moderation, too. I always park as close as I can get! Hiking in from the parking lot, I didn't notice her truck. Maybe she had to park further away than I thought.

The restaurant wasn't crowded and as I approached the nicely decorated desk, I told the hostess I was waiting for another person. I asked, if by chance, if Doctor Shannon was already here. She scanned the waiting list, but didn't see her name. I gave her my name and took a seat while I waited for Aubrey to arrive. I was early and she probably was caught in traffic. It didn't matter that I needed to wait for her.

Gazing out the window, I noticed what I thought was her truck pulling into the parking lot. Ever so slightly, pulling around each corner of the lot looking desperately for a spot to park. Finally, half way down the aisle, I saw her whip into a parking space. She must have cut the corner too close. She backed up slightly and then pulled forward, as if she were straightening the wheels to align her truck between the lines. Getting out of the truck, I watched her walk through the parking lot and onto the sidewalk, where eventually I saw her enter the restaurant. I noticed as she stopped at the hostess desk, and apparently asked if one of our names were on the waiting list. I saw the hostess point in my direction and she soon arrived at the table.

"I hope I'm not late! I got here as soon as I could...the traffic is horrible!"

"No, you're fine...you're not late. Is everything okay?"

"Everything is fine. I left the office on time, but then I ran into traffic on the four lane. It must have been everyone's time to eat lunch at noon today! I didn't think I would find a parking space either. Where did you have to park?"

"In the back-forty! It doesn't matter, though. It was time for me to start my new exercise program anyway! Besides, the holidays are rapidly approaching and everyone is probably trying to get some early Christmas shopping in."

We both had a laugh over the parking situation and then decided to order our drinks.

"How do you feel today? Are you still feeling sluggish?"

"Unfortunately, I am. I even overslept this morning, which is very unusual for me. But, I did take the prenatal vitamin and I am feeling somewhat better. I guess that means I'll be able to tolerate the iron in these pills. I think I'm even ready to shop!"

"If you like, we can leave your car here and travel around in mine today. Afterwards, we can swing back by and pick up your car. Is that okay with you?"

I admired the way she always asked me if her decisions were okay with me. Made me feel as though she was thinking ahead and looking out for me. She's beginning to make me feel special. Besides, I think she likes looking out for my best interest. She knows I'm new at this pregnancy thing...

"That's fine with me. There's really no sense in taking two cars...especially if we're going to the same places, right?"

"Right! And besides, driving all over the city today may wear you out a little, especially with the holiday drivers. I don't want you to get too tired. If you start feeling sluggish today, you just let me know and we'll stop."

"Oh, I'll be fine. Besides, I have a lot to accomplish today. After I eat lunch, I'll be ready."

"I just don't want you to overdo it. What we don't accomplish today there will be other days to catch up where we left off."

The waitress brought us our drinks and then we ordered our lunch.

"Listen Aubrey, I wanted to ask you a question about my pregnancy...is it true that if you read to your baby, before he is born, that he can hear you?"

"Studies have shown that, yes. Why do you ask?"

"My mother told me that she read to me while she was pregnant. I guess I just wanted to know for sure and not something she made up."

"Well, it's true. May I see the book?"

I handed her the storybook my mother had passed down to me. I watched her eyes as she read page by page. When she finished it, she smiled, closed the book and returned it to me.

"What an amazing children's book. She has handed this down to you for you to read to your child?"

"Yes, she did. I loved that book as a child and I think my son will enjoy it too. Don't you?"

"Of course he will." She looked away and stared off into another direction. I reached for her hand across the table and held it.

"Aubrey? What is it...what's wrong?"

She looked at me with tears in her eyes. I could tell something was terribly wrong. I could feel it in my gut as if my sixth sense was screaming.

"Katie is in town... She called to tell me she wants to get back together."

My heart suddenly stopped beating for what felt like an eternity. Did I hear her correctly? Oh my God, this is so insane. I felt like a bomb had just been dropped in my life. I looked at her in disbelief. The one person who had abused her obviously wanted another chance.

"Katie...is in town...and she wants to get back together with you? What did you tell her?"

"I told her no and that I didn't want any more contact with her. I can't believe she wants to come back in to my life! Since she called me, I am terrified. I don't want to be anywhere near her. I don't want her near you or me. I know she has probably gone through some therapy and AA, but that is no reason for her to assume I will be a part of her life now. I want no part of it or her games. Tell me something...would you get back with Annie after what you have gone through to try and get over her and the past?"

I thought about her question for a moment and realized how much it would hurt me if Annie had tried to contact me again. Because of how I feel about Aubrey, there's no way I could get back together with Annie. Aubrey is different and I know she cares about me in every way and just not because of the pregnancy.

"No Aubrey, there's no way I could go back. I have a new life now and for the moment, it has meaning. As long as you're in my life, that's where I want to stay. You have made these past few weeks the happiest I have been in a long time. Without you, none of this would be possible. You are in my life for a reason and for whatever the reason, I'm glad. Aubrey, you make me happy, not Annie. If you chose to go back right now to Katie, I would try and understand. I may not like it very much, but I would try. I feel that we have something between us. Don't you?"

She reached across the table and gently took my hand in hers. With tears in her eyes, she smiled that beautiful smile and it made my heart skip a beat. She looked at me and shook her head. In the softness of her voice, I finally heard the words.

"I'm not going anywhere. I'm exactly where I want to be...and yes, we do have something between us. It was Katie's call that made me realize how I would feel if you were no longer in my life. I look forward to our luncheons, your office visits, and our time alone together. I would miss out on a lot if..."

"Don't even go there! I'm not sure I could handle another rejection at this moment. Listen, we have both been through so much and there's no room for any more negativity. I mean, we...have so much to look forward to, don't we? What I'm trying to say is that I'm over three months pregnant, thanks to you. You have been a very positive influence in my life. Not only that, but I want you to share this whole baby experience with me. I have wanted to tell you that for a few weeks now. But, I wasn't sure how you felt. I need someone in my life who is positive, stable, professional, spiritual, and feels the same connection. You are all of that Aubrey. I want you and only you in my life, not Annie."

The waitress brought our food, but I don't think either of us were very hungry by this point. I knew I needed to eat, but I was too anxious from the conversation.

"You know, since I first took you home from the office I knew we had something special. I wished I could've seen your face when you realized I had a rainbow flag on the rear window of my truck! I was hoping you saw it. I wanted you to know...I wanted you to know that I was interested to you."

"First of all, if you would've seen me standing in the driveway with my mouth wide open in awe from what I saw, you would've laughed all the way home! In fact, I came up with an excuse if one of my neighbors would have asked me what I was doing standing out in the middle of my driveway, covered in snow."

"What was your excuse?"

"I would've told them I was catching snowflakes!" Laughing, I felt my face blush as I told her my flimsy excuse and I wondered what she was thinking.

"Second of all and on a serious note, I don't doubt your ethical values. I don't believe you are the type of person who takes their client's home with them. I don't see that in you. What I do see is a person who takes pride in their work, clients, friends, family, and community. I can tell you are very dedicated."

Both of us had picked at our meals until we were sure we'd had enough. We were ready to shop! This afternoon could have turned into a disaster I thought. But instead, the conversation turned into a wonderful insight for us both by how we communicated to each other how we felt. I was relieved she wasn't going back to Katie. She obviously felt comfortable enough to tell me the truth about Katie's phone call and I am thankful for her honesty. She could have lied and told me other reasons for not wanting to continue our relationship, but she didn't. She stayed true to her feelings and revealed the truth. I believe we conveyed our feelings to each other today for a reason. I think we had come to that point where we really wanted each other to know. True, Katie instigated the conversation, but in the end we let each other know how we felt. Personally, I was glad I told her what I did...I could have told her more, but for now it was enough.

Leaving the restaurant, we climbed into her truck and left. Oh, how I want to know more...

"The shop I told you about is not far from here. Are you still feeling up to shopping?"

"Of course! I can't wait to start finding some bargains. I do need to get my maternity clothes in order...I only have a few pieces of clothing left that fit comfortably."

"I promise, you will have more to choose from than any other store in town. They not only have clothes, but also baby furniture and accessories your baby might need. I know your family has brought over some clothes, but what else will you need? What about a crib or car seat?"

"Well, they did bring over a crib, but I don't have the car seat..."

"By the way, are you registered anywhere yet...I mean for a baby shower?"

"Actually, I was just thinking about that just a few days ago. If there were any person who would do that it would be my baby sister, Jackie. But, unfortunately she's out of state. I'll have to call her to find out when she's coming in for a visit. If she can't come in except for the delivery, then I'll have to come up with plan 'B'."

"What do you mean you'll have to come up with plan 'B'? Why should you have to do anything? This is for you and the baby. First, let me know what your sister is going to do and we'll go from there, okay?"

"I know my family...and I know they'll want to be a part of this. Especially my mother. That's why I'd rather Jackie been in control of this shower. Don't get me wrong, I think my mother has good intentions and she wants only what's good for her daughters. Sometimes, a family can be too involved, that's all. It's not that I don't appreciate their efforts or being there for me, because I do. It's just...I'm ready to start my own family. Does that make sense?"

"Of course it does. And I understand, believe me. Just let me know about Jackie's intentions, okay?"

"I promise, I will as soon as I hear from her."

We pulled into the second-hand store, parking lot and walked in. She was right. The store was huge and full of everything I needed for my baby and me. I felt like a kid in candy store! The racks were full of clothes that looked as though they had never been worn. Name brands like Liz Claiborne, Tommy Hilfiger, Bass, Land's End and others that caught my eye. I couldn't believe the choices and quality of clothing that was here, not to mention the baby accessories. I turned around to see where Aubrey was in the store and she was right on my heals, struggling to keep up. I stopped for a minute and began to laugh. She looked at me like I was crazy. Then, she began laughing! We stood in the middle of the store, laughing hysterically, until we cried! Tears were streaming down our faces. She had no idea why I was laughing, but I didn't care. At that moment, she was priceless. She had no idea I could shop like this. I was so excited, I couldn't help myself. Going from rack to rack, I began throwing clothes in the cart and before long, I had made a huge pile, overflowing on all sides. All I had to do now was try them all on!

V.A. Buck

Chapter 18

We left the store with more bags than I could carry. She opened up the hatch of her sport utility and started stacking and cramming in more and more bags until the hatch could barely close. We laughed as we forced the hatch down! We climbed in her truck again and off we went to the next stop...my place. I wanted to show her all the baby things my family had passed down to me.

"Are you thirsty?"

"Yes...can we stop and get something?"

"Of course...all that shopping made me thirsty! By the way, I'll need to make one stop before we get to your place...is that okay with you?"

"Sure, no problem."

We pulled into a nearby convenient store and she hopped out.

"What would you like, my treat."

"How about a twenty ounce Hawaiian Punch?"

She smiled, turned and started walking toward the door. I noticed her faded blue jeans and how sexy she looked while she walked. She filled them out nicely, with just a slight sway in her hips. Her hair bounced off her shoulders as she walked. I wondered why she didn't have it pulled back in a braid today. It didn't matter though, she was beautiful no matter how her hair was fixed or what she wore. She started walking back toward the truck. Her jacket unzipped, I could make out the outline of her bra through her white Tommy shirt. Her shirt, unbuttoned two buttons down, was neatly tucked in her jeans. It had been pulled out slightly as it barely hung over her jeans' button. I couldn't see her breasts, but the outline of her bra revealed they were firm. I could only imagine... My thoughts were abruptly interrupted when she climbed back into the truck. She handed me my drink and I thanked her. I watched her as we drove down through town. Sitting beside her, I glanced at her shirt in hopes of a closer look. Nothing more than what I had seen before. I kept watching her. Finally, she looked over at me.

"You're awfully quiet. Are you okay?"

"Yes, I'm fine. I was just thinking about something." I hoped she wouldn't ask me...I could feel my face start to blush about my fascination over her breasts.

"Care to share?"

"Uh, well...I'm not sure you really want to know what I'm thinking right now." She kept looking at me and must have noticed my red face...it never fails! It's a dead give-away for me when I get embarrassed.

"I'm listening...go ahead, try me." She started to smile and I started to squirm. Oh God...I should've lied! What am I going to say now? Do I tell her the truth that I was staring at her breasts...hoping to get a closer look? No!

"I was just admiring your...uh, well...the way you're dressed today. I think you look very... sexy in what you have on."

"Really? Sexy?"

I was taken back by her reaction to my answer. It left me with the impression that maybe she didn't feel very sexy in what she was wearing.

"Yes Aubrey...you look very sexy in what you have on! You don't think you're sexy?"

I studied her face and now she looked as though she was getting embarrassed.

"It's just that...you caught me by surprise...because I wasn't trying to be sexy. This is just my casual look. Don't get me wrong, I'm flattered you think so! Thank you for the compliment."

Oh, I could compliment her all right...but I had said all I needed to for now.

"Don't forget, I need to make one stop before we get to your place, okay?"

"That's fine."

She continued driving toward my place when she took a turn into Summer Field Estates. It was out near the lake and in a fairly new subdivision. It was only about three miles from my place. Most of the houses out here were huge, colonial brick homes with what looked like acre-front yards. I had to travel this way sometimes whenever I needed to go to the post office. I think I had only driven through the subdivision once or twice while house hunting. Clearly, out of my price range. I enjoyed the views though. As she drove slowly along the street, I admired the huge homes, with neatly mowed and trimmed lush lawns. They were nicely landscaped with perennials and annuals flawlessly spaced throughout, edging mailbox sites and foundations. Made me feel we were a part of an historical site.

Most every house in the subdivision was wonderfully decorated with the spirit of Christmas. Lights streamed from the eaves and gutters of houses as garland was draped neatly along the banisters and railings of porches. Wreathes were placed methodically in the center of the exterior doorways, beckoning family, neighbors' and anyone else who cared to share the true spirit of Christmas. You could see their Christmas trees, centered in front of the picture window, decorated from top to bottom with ornaments, icicles, and bright lights. The decoration schemes would remind you of an old fashion Christmas, somewhere in the south. All we needed now was snow. She finally pulled into a driveway and opened her door.

"Come on and get out. I want to show you something."

I opened my door and got out. The garage door slowly opened and she walked in, motioning me to follow her. Cautiously, I did. She opened the side door into the house and she walked in, in front of me. I looked down and saw a huge, but beautiful longhaired, tabby cat come running toward us. I stopped dead in my tracks as I watched her pick it up and give it a big kiss on it's nose.

"Meet Jasper."

"Is he what you wanted to show me? He's beautiful!"

"Well, he's only part of what I wanted to show you. Come on, let me give you a tour..."

I had no idea where we were, but I was up for a tour. Standing in the kitchen, it was gorgeous. An all tile floor, white appliances, solid surface countertops and beautiful hickory cabinets. Even the kitchen faucet was top of the line. From the kitchen, she opened the sliding glass doors and walked out onto the patio where a pool appeared. Off to the side, a diving board. On the other side, a patio table, with a market umbrella and chairs to match. The umbrella had white Christmas lights draped around the edges and then wrapped downward, around and around the pole until it finally stopped. Even the fence surrounding the landscaped back yard was streamed with white lights as well. Even though the pool was covered, you could tell it had been well maintained.

We reentered the house and she took me into the living room, where I saw a huge Christmas tree. The tree, centered in front of a picture window, was decorated in all old fashion and hand made ornaments. White lights adorned each and every branch and silvery icicles dangled from the ends of branches. The icicles glistened whenever Jasper would walk underneath a branch, catching his tail on it and making the icicle shimmer. His whiskers would twitch every time he rubbed against one. On the opposite wall from the tree, a fireplace. The mantle was decorated with fresh pine greenery, stockings, and votive candles. We left the living room and entered the den. Following her through the arched opening, we then came to a winding staircase, which led up. The handrail of the staircase was eloquently wrapped in garland, natural pinecone, poinsettia, and beautifully tied Christmas bows. It looked like something out of a Southern Living Magazine. I followed her without a sound as Jasper was close on my heels. At the top of the stairway, she turned left into a beautifully decorated bedroom. The bedroom furniture was something out of a Thomasville catalog. Very elegantly dressed with a comforter, pillows and shams. Even the curtains matched! She walked a few feet away and opened another door that revealed a master bath. Peeking in, I first saw the garden tub. Above it, a skylight. I was speechless. I continued to follow her throughout the house and when we were through I was starting to get tired. Confused, I didn't understand why we she had brought me here. Perhaps she knew the owner or maybe she was house sitting for one of her doctor friends. I was getting curious as she started feeding Jasper.

"Aubrey, whose house is this?"

Putting down the can of cat food, she turned around and smiled at me.

"Welcome to my home Terri. What do you think?"

"Excuse me? Did you say...your house?"

Suddenly, I felt off-balance...

V.A. Buck

Chapter 18

"Terri... Terri, are you okay?"

It felt like something or someone kept trying to pry my eyes open. I was so sleepy and tired...my arms limp and I had that feeling like I was drunk. I fought to open my eyes, but they were closed tight, as if a clamp had been placed over them. What was happening?

"This is Doctor Aubrey Shannon. I have a thirty-nine year old, white, pregnant female who has fainted. Blood pressure is one hundred thirty-five over one hundred, pulse is eighty and respiration's, shallow. Skin is cool and clammy. I don't see any obvious injuries. The address is four twenty-two Summer Field Street in Summer Field Estates. Yes, I'll wait until the ambulance gets here."

I was fading in and out of a sleep and words were just not registering...everything was blurry. I felt something cool on my forehead, with drops of coolness dripping down my neck onto my shirt. Nothing was making sense. My mind was weaving back and forth from unfamiliar images. Forcing myself to focus...and trying to remember...I wasn't getting anywhere. My head was hurting, but so was my mouth. I tasted blood. What was happening to me?

"Terri.... Terri, can you hear me? If you can, squeeze my hand."

I could hear her voice. I could feel her hand. I focused hard to squeeze...with all the strength I had, I squeezed her hand.

"Okay, now I know you can hear me. Listen to me, carefully. You have fainted and looks as though you have hit your head and bit your tongue. I want you to lie very still and try not to move. The ambulance is on the way. We are taking you to the hospital to make sure everything is okay. I will be right here beside you."

I heard what she was saying. I squeezed her hand again. There was no way I could move. I felt lifeless. I kept waiting for her to say something, but she didn't. All I could hear were the sirens from the ambulance.

"The ambulance is here. I need to go out and meet them. I'll be right back."

I could hear footsteps moving quickly across the floor. I heard her open the door and let out a yell. The sirens stopped...they must be here.

"What's her name?"

"Terri"

"Terri, can you hear me?"

"She has been squeezing my hand indicating she heard me."

I felt another hand take mine.

"Terri, can you hear me?"

I squeezed as hard as I could that I heard him.

"Can you open your eyes for me?"

I lay lifeless...I couldn't move anything. I felt his hand on my face and soon he opened one of my eyes and I could see a blurry image of a man.

"Did you check for a fetal heartbeat since she fainted?"

"No, I was concerned about the head injury."

"Okay, I'll check and see if I can hear anything."

I felt something placed on top of my belly, moving slowly and at intervals. I heard nothing. I kept waiting for someone to say something, but no one did.

"Let's get her onto a back board and in the ambulance. We need to transport her to the Medical Center. We'll go ahead and start an IV and administer saline. Let's get her on oxygen too."

I felt a swift prick in my arm and I felt my arm jerk.

They put an oxygen mask over my face, placed me on a backboard and into the ambulance. I heard the sirens. Where was Aubrey?

~

"Oh my head…. Aubrey…"

"I'm here Terri…."

"What…happened? Where am I?"

"You fainted and now you're in the hospital. How do you feel?"

"My head hurts like hell….can't I get anything for this pain? Why does my head hurt so badly?"

"When you fainted, you fell and hit your head…bit your tongue pretty badly, too. They've just given you something for the pain. It should ease up pretty soon."

"Oh God…what about the baby….is he okay?"

"The baby is fine… We're more concerned about you right now."

I could hear it in her voice that something was wrong.

"Why…what's going on?"

"You apparently fainted because of low blood sugar… What's the last thing you remember?"

"Let me think for a second. I remember you giving me a tour of a house...Jasper...cat food...and feeling really tired after the tour."

"Anything else?"

"Not at the moment... Why?"

"Did you eat all of your lunch?"

"Not that I can remember."

"That's why you fainted. You didn't eat enough for you and the baby. When we shopped and then went to the house for the tour, you over did things a bit I'm afraid."

"Oh...am I going to be okay?"

"As of right now, yes. You've got a couple of stitches in your head, along with a couple of IV's going in each arm. One IV is an antibiotic, to rid the possibility of infection from the cuts, and the other IV is a saline solution to help restore your blood sugar back within normal limits. Your blood sugar dropped to a dangerous level. We'll need to keep an eye on this as you get closer to you delivery date."

"Did you call any of my family?"

"No, I didn't. Should I have?"

"As long as you were here with me, it doesn't matter now. I'll tell them later. You're sure I'm going to be okay...I mean, with the baby?"

"Yes, everything will be fine as long as we maintain your caloric intake to feed both you and the baby. We'll keep a watchful eye, I promise."

"Aubrey, are you sure the baby is okay..."

"Don't worry, he's fine. Try and get some rest. They're going to monitor you overnight and then you can go home in the morning. Want me to call your family now?"

"Are you going to stay with me?"

"Do you want me to stay?"

"Well, if you have something you need to do, you don't have to stay..."

"I'll tell you what...I'll call your family, let them know what's happened. They can spend some time with you and after they leave, I'll come back and stay with you. Okay?"

She smiled and put her hand on my forehead and brushed my hair away from my face.

"Okay, that's fine...I just don't....I just don't want to be left alone...I'm afraid something might happen."

"I'll call them now so that they can come on up. I'll stay until they get here."

"Aubrey, thanks for taking such good care of me. I don't know what I would've done if you hadn't been there when it happened."

She dialed my parents phone number and apparently mom answered. I heard Aubrey explaining what had happened and soon, she hung up the phone. Every thing happened so fast. The last thing I remember was feeling funny. I don't remember hitting the floor or anything. It's weird...almost like I blacked-out.

"They're on their way. I'll stay with you until they get here and then I'll leave. They won't be able to spend a lot of time with you, but I'll let them know what time visiting hour's end. Then, I'll come back and stay. I'll make sure you get the rest you need."

"I'm sure you will."

"Terri, you really gave me a scare tonight. I'm just glad you... and of course the baby are going to be okay. I'm thankful I was there when it happened, too. You both could've been in serious trouble if I hadn't."

"Now you're scaring me... What did you tell my mother?"

"I told her exactly what happened...that you fainted from low blood sugar, hit you head and bit your tongue, and you were in the hospital for overnight observation. You would probably be able to go home in the morning if your blood sugar levels were back within normal levels."

"Did you tell her where I was when it happened..."

"No, it wasn't important. All that's important is your child and yourself right now. Where you were shouldn't matter. If they ask, it will be up to you if you want to explain your whereabouts."

She was right. But, I don't remember where I was really. I was in someone's house, but I don't know whose. It wasn't long before mom and dad arrived and stayed by my side. Aubrey was sitting in one of the chairs across from the bed, keeping a watchful eye. I drifted in and out of sleep while they stayed. Just knowing someone was there made me feel more comfortable. Aubrey had left by this point, but I knew she would be back soon. I was glad she would be back to get me through the night. I trusted her so much. I don't know what I would've done if she hadn't been there to call an ambulance. I guess I would still be lying on the floor. I hope one day, I can look back on this and be amused. Somehow, I doubted it since I put my child in jeopardy.

I certainly never meant any harm by not eating my lunch. Besides, who knew? Not only that, but who was hungry after hearing Katie wanted Aubrey back. It was enough to make my stomach churn. I'm glad to know she's happy with me and we can start working on a more serious relationship now. She would make sure my baby and me were okay from here on out. Quite frankly, I was glad to know I had help on the way...not only from my parents, but also from her. I obviously had a lot to learn from this pregnancy and I welcomed the help. I just thought I could do this alone, without any help. Now, maybe not.

Maybe I did learn something from that Red-Tail Hawk...keeping a watchful eye over his mate while she prepared the nest. I suppose not even the best of us can do it alone without some kind of help. I had to accept that. It's not that I wasn't strong, caring, or even that I had failed in some way about this pregnancy. It was the fact that I had to acknowledge I didn't know it all and obviously, had no clue what I was about to go through. Plain and simple, I needed the help. I knew I wasn't going to be alone tonight and I was thankful.

Mom and dad had left by now and Aubrey had returned, faithfully, to stay with me throughout the night. I could go home tomorrow morning and start a brand new day.

V.A. Buck

Chapter 19

Leaving the hospital was such a relief. I couldn't wait to get home. Not only had my spirit been lifted, but also my awareness. Aubrey had made me aware of the dangers to my health and the health of my baby. She had a keen way about her that made me want to listen. I knew I had to be careful now. I couldn't risk another hospital bout. No matter how long I was there, I didn't like the feeling of things being out of my control. I felt like I was in good hands now.

Pulling into my driveway, my car was nowhere to be found. Then, I remembered I left it at the restaurant.

"Aubrey, I need to go and get my car from the restaurant. I hope they didn't have it towed away."

"I hope you didn't mind, but I made arrangements with your dad to have it brought here for you. They should be bringing it some time today. Besides, you have nowhere to go, do you?"

"You're right, I don't need to go anywhere. Thanks for doing that. But, when did you and dad discuss that anyway?"

"While you were sleeping at the hospital last night."

"Oh, okay. I am so glad to be home...and I'm getting hungry too!"

"That's a good sign! How's your head? Does it still hurt?"

"A little, but not too badly. I can tolerate it."

"You can take some Tylenol or Ibuprofen if it continues. It won't hurt the baby."

"Good, I'll go ahead and take some now to try and get it under control."

"Do you have anything to fix for breakfast?"

"Well, there should be some eggs, bacon, sausage, bread, cereal...help yourself."

"Great, what do you feel like eating for breakfast?"

"I could probably eat some scrambled eggs and sausage, why?"

"I'm fixing breakfast...if you don't mind me in your kitchen?"

"Are you serious? You don't have to do that!"

"I know I don't...I want to."

"Really? You would fix me breakfast?"

"Of course, why wouldn't I?"

"I...I don't know. You've already done so much Aubrey. I feel guilty, I guess."

"Feel guilty? Why in the world should you feel guilty?"

"I guess because it seems you're always doing something nice for me lately. What have I done for you?"

"Oh for God's sake...would you stop? Do you not want to be taken care of when you are sick? Look, I'm sure you would do the same for me if I were in the same predicament. Right?"

"Okay, okay...I get the message. And yes, I would do the same for you."

"Why don't you go and get in a hot shower and by the time you are through, breakfast should be ready. It will make you feel better."

Grabbing some clean clothes, I headed toward the shower and closed the door behind me. She was right, a hot shower would help. If I didn't know any better, I'd say she already knew me. How strange is this... I barely know her, but I feel as though she knows me inside and out. Am I that transparent? Maybe I wanted her to know me that well. Only Annie knew me this well.

Trying to forget yesterday's events, I stood in the shower, feeling the pulsating water beating against my tired back. She was right, it felt relaxing and well worth the wait. All I needed now was a massage, but I'd settle for breakfast. I stood in the shower for what seemed like eternity and decided I'd had enough. I slipped into some comfortable clothes and opened the door to an aroma only one would smell coming from either a country inn or bed and breakfast. It smelled absolutely incredible. It made me even hungrier.

I took my clothes I had worn home from the hospital, and placed them in my hamper in the bedroom. I turned around to find Aubrey asleep in my bed. I was so taken by her beauty that I just stood still for a moment and stared. I was afraid to move...I didn't want to wake her silent dreams. She looked so peaceful lying there. I found a throw and covered her carefully. Walking out of the bedroom, I closed the door slightly behind me. I felt guilty eating without her, but I didn't want to wake her. I knew she must have been exhausted from the whole ordeal at the hospital.

I finished my breakfast and went back to check on her and she was still sound asleep. I watched her for a moment and while my thoughts took me back to the convenient store, I remembered how sexy she looked in her faded jeans and white Tommy shirt. Here she is...lying in my bed. I walked over to the other side of the bed and gently crawled in beside her, trying not to disturb her deep sleep. I don't know where my thoughts or boldness were coming from... I just wanted to be beside her and hold her. I wanted to know how it felt again...to hold someone I cared about. Sliding closer and closer to her body, I struggled to be quiet and motionless. She didn't move. Finally beside her, our bodies touching, I put my arm across her body and laid my head on her shoulder. I held her close to me. I could smell her perfume and how soft her skin felt against mine. As I lay there with her soft hair touching my face, I was reminded of the night she was last here, standing in front of the fireplace. I closed my eyes and let the smell of her perfume and the softness of her skin transpires me into a different world. It was as if my heart started to beat again...my soul stirring, and my spirit rekindled for the first time since I returned home. What had she done to me? Was I falling in-love with her?

I knew I was very attracted to her...she was all I ever thought about. I wanted to touch her in a way I knew would make her crazy. I wanted to take her to new heights she had never been. I wanted to kiss her passionately. I even envisioned our first kiss weeks ago and thought about how it made me feel. So warm and gentle. I wanted her to the feel the passion and let her know just how sexy I thought she really was... I could feel my face and neck burning up...whew, I had to stop thinking about this sexy stuff! She was driving me crazy. Should I wake her from her dreams?

I could feel my heart pounding. I raised up and looked down at her. Slowly, I leaned down and put my lips on hers, kissing her gently and softly. As I pulled away, she opened her eyes. I didn't move away, but kept looking down into her eyes. Hers were searching mine desperately for answers. I slowly leaned down once more and kissed her lips again, only to find her kissing me back. Her mouth began slowly opening more until her tongue reached mine. Her arms wrapped around my body tightly and pulled me down on her. I could feel her heart pounding against my chest. I could feel our kisses were getting harder and harder until our tongues felt intertwined. I could feel myself getting wet. I pulled away and looked at her for some answers of my own. She sat up and started unbuttoning her shirt. I remembered the outline of her bra through her shirt and wondered how firm her breasts would be...she pulled off her shirt and unhooked her bra. Her dark skin accented her breasts. They were perfect and her nipples, erect. She took my hand and placed it on one of her breasts, slowly moving it to where only my fingers were slightly touching her nipple. I watched her as she closed her eyes and laid her head back. Softly moaning, she pulled her hand away from mine as if to let me take control. I leaned down on her and placed my mouth over her breast and started to lick her nipple...first lightly and then quickly in motion. She began to move the rest of her body in rhythm with me. Her body soft and slim, I slowly started unbuttoning her jeans and then removing them along with her thong panties. She took my hand and placed it on her soft, short hairs and stroked them slightly...then pushing my hand down. She was so warm and wet...I could feel her body jerk as I lightly stroked across her clitoris and then moved back down to her wetness. With her hand on mine, she pushed me inside her and I heard her soft moan as I slowly pulled out and then pushed back inside. With everything inside of me, I wanted to feel her climax. I wanted to hear her moan for more. As I lay on top her, our bodies were moving to the rhythm like a metronome keeping time. I could feel her getting closer and closer until I felt her close tightly around my wet fingers and then...relaxing. I held her close and laid my head on her shoulder.

Feeling her close to me, I took a deep breath and sighed. I'd never imagined she would feel that wonderful. I stroked her hair, hoping it would relax her back to sleep. Holding her close to me, I could feel her body relax and soon she fell back to sleep.

V.A. Buck

Chapter 20

Waking up beside her the next morning was the best feeling in the world. Still asleep, I left her lying there and got up to make breakfast. All I could think about was how incredible she made me feel. Making love to her last night was totally unexpected. I had no idea where the impulse came from, but I was glad it happened. Now, maybe we can move forward to the next step. It didn't matter to me that she didn't try to touch me. I wanted to touch and caress her. I wanted to make her feel special...the way she makes me feel when we are together. Maybe now, this relationship will finally start to grow and blossom into something more meaningful.

Starting breakfast, I tried to be quiet with the pots and pans clanging. It's not always easy trying to unhook a fry pan from another without making any noise. The smell of bacon cooking reminded me of when I was younger and my mom would fix us breakfast. I knew it wouldn't be long before I would fix it for my own child. I actually looked forward to the many breakfast's I would cook for my own family. I turned around to grab a potholder and noticed her there standing in the doorway of my bedroom. I watched her as she fumbled with my robe, trying to place it around her without revealing what was beneath. Tying a knot in the belt of my robe, she glanced up and caught me watching her.

She walked over to me and put her arms around my neck and kissed me softly. Closing my eyes, I held her close. I could smell her perfume and it took me back to last night as I laid my head on her shoulder. I could feel how soft her hair felt against my face. What a wonderful feeling. Letting her arms unwrap from around me, I looked in her eyes and I could see what she was feeling. It was as if she revealed her soul. I haven't seen that look in a long time.

Making her breakfast was something of a first for me. It was like we were starting a family...I hoped we were anyway. We spent the day together talking and laughing and just relaxing. We even started decorating my house with the Christmas spirit. This was quality time together. I learned more about her today than I ever hoped. Talking about her practice, listening to Christmas music, looking at photo albums, and petting the cats. What a wonderful day. I had needed this for such a long time. I knew now she needed me.

We continued to spend some time together for weeks after that special night. But not like I had hoped. The Christmas holidays were right around the corner and I hoped we could spend some time together during the holidays. I also missed the intimacy. I knew she had been quite busy with her practice, but I felt like I had not seen her in forever. I couldn't help but think that something was wrong.

I had another appointment with her today and hopefully, she would be able to tell me. Walking into her clinic, I sat and listened to holiday music until it was time to see her. Escorted once again down the hall and back into the examining room, I was eager to find out the sex of my child. I still hoped for a son. She soon entered my room.

"How have you been feeling? Any more symptoms of feeling faint?"

"Actually, no. I have been eating several meals a day and taking my prenatal vitamins faithfully."

"Okay, lets take a look and see if we can determine the sex of your baby. Just lie back and I'll put some gel on your belly for the sonogram."

She raised my gown slightly and placed the gel on my belly and began the procedure with the sonogram. Watching the monitor with her, I could see my baby. She began to point to different parts of the baby, showing me the legs, arms, fingers, and toes and the umbilical cord. The baby was turned slightly, as to not reveal anything we wanted to see. We could see however, that the baby was sucking its thumb. I watched the monitor in amazement. I never knew that I would actually be able to see such tiny and delicate little features of my baby. This tiny and precious human being, growing inside of me, was a true gift from God. How blessed I felt to be able to carry this child. My dream was coming true. All I had to do was hold on to it...hold on for dear life. My family was giving me support, I had a wonderful new friend and a baby growing inside of me. They always say, "be careful what you ask for." All I've wanted is a family of my own...and now I'm about to have it. With everything inside of me, this is what I want.

Lying on the table, she had completed the procedure. She listened to the baby's heartbeat, took my blood pressure, and felt my pulse.

"Everything is within normal limits...the baby's heartbeat is strong. Do you have any questions?"

"By what you've seen and heard, what do you think the baby's sex is...girl or boy?"

"Well, it's hard to tell without actually seeing anything on the monitor...and I don't want to give you any false hope. I don't know what your baby will be for sure. Let me ask you this...will it make any difference what it is as long as it's healthy?

"Well, of course not...it's just that...I'm not sure I would know how to raise a daughter. I know I would have no problems raising a son...does that sound crazy?"

"Terri, of course not. Most of us have our preferences as to what we want the child to be...I just don't want you to be devastated if you don't have what you prefer. Do you understand what I mean by that?"

"Yes, of course. I can learn what I need to for the sake of my child...if I don't have a son, I mean. I have two sisters who can help and of course my mom...and you can help, too?"

"I thought you'd never ask... Of course I will. You know that!" She said that as she smiled her wonderfully big, beautiful smile.

"Speaking of sisters, have you contacted Jackie yet?"

"Oh my God... I totally forgot! I will do that as soon as I get home from here. Listen, there's one other thing I wanted to ask you... I know this is probably not the place or time to ask you this, but were you okay with the other night? I mean, with you spending the night with me?"

I watched her as she started fidgeting with instruments lying on a stainless steel tray beside my examining table. She turned away from me so that I couldn't see her face. Now, it felt like something was really wrong. My stomach turned over and over until I could feel it starting to churn on its own. Oh no...

"It was...totally unexpected and I was so tired...I've felt so guilty for not attending to your needs."

"You're avoiding my question, aren't you?"

She began to walk away from my side when she turned around to face me.

"No, not really... Let's see...how can I put this..."

"Oh God...you weren't okay with it."

"It was totally unexpected and yes, I was okay with all of it. In fact, I've never been so sure about anything in my life as I was with the other night. You are so genuine, caring, loving, and gentle. I loved everything about that night, except...

Oh no, here it comes...

"Except, that I didn't get to show you how I felt... I'm sorry we haven't been able to spend quality time together like we did...but I've felt so guilty about this that I wasn't sure how to approach you about it."

"Aubrey, you can tell me anything. Don't avoid me about the subject, just tell me what's on your mind. I don't bite...at least not hard."

I tried to lighten the conversation a little, but I could tell something was on her mind.

"I tell you what, why don't we meet at my place tonight and we can talk about it then...is that okay with you?"

"Of course, except for one thing..."

"What's that?"

"Where do you live?"

"What do you mean, where do I live? Wait a minute, you really don't remember, do you?"

"Remember what?"

"Remember the tour I gave you of the house and Jasper, the cat?"

"Faintly...why?"

"Terri, that house is mine. Do you remember how we got there?"

"You mean, directions? Maybe...I'm not sure. I think so...but, you better write down some directions, just in case I get lost."

"Okay, no problem. I think you'll remember once you get in the neighborhood. Just be there at seven sharp..."

Still lying there on the table, with gel on my belly, I was stunned. I couldn't believe I had been in her house and didn't know it! That must have been the night I passed out! No wonder I didn't remember... What in the world was I thinking! I felt so embarrassed. Oh well, I guess I could've really said something stupid about the house. Thank God I didn't. Hopefully tonight, I won't pass out on the kitchen floor again! Damn I need a glass of wine and about a pack of cigarettes. Where is my brain? I have to remember when I get home that I needed to call Jackie before I went to her house at seven.

~

Jackie's answering machine came on and left the typical recording for me to leave my message after the beep.

"Beep."

"Hey, it's me...everything is fine...call me when you get in... I love ya."

I finally remembered to get in touch with her about the baby shower. I just felt as though I was running out of time. There just didn't seem to be enough hours in the day to get everything accomplished. I still had Christmas shopping left to do for my family and for Aubrey. How in the world was I going to feel when the baby came? Overwhelmed, I suppose! At least I knew I had help on the way. The only problem was that I didn't know the sex of my child. If I at least knew that, I could start getting the baby's room ready...with the appropriate colors. I guess if I had to, I could do everything in a neutral color. Then, tie it all in with either blues or yellows or pinks. God, I hate pink. I hope I don't have to color coordinate in pinks...

Yellow I can deal with and blue is one of my favorite colors. So, those won't be a problem.

I walked across to the second bedroom and stared at the messy room. This was the junk room. I had everything in here from Christmas decorations to my weight-lifting equipment. I was going to have to do some weeding out or have a garage sale or something... What was I going to do? At least I can take my decorations out of the room. I guess I would have to figure it out later. Right now, I had to start making a list of everything I needed for the baby and it's room. I grabbed a legal pad and started writing down numbers on the left side of the page when the phone rang.

"Hello?"

"Terri! Hi, it's Jackie! Did you call earlier?"

"Hey you! Yeah, it wasn't too long ago."

"I guess I was in the shower when you called. Is everything okay?"

"Yes, all is well on the home front. Listen, the reason I called is about a baby shower... Will you be in town for it? Aubrey and I were wondering."

"When do you plan on having it?"

"I'm not sure yet. Will you be able to fly in for the holidays or just for the shower?"

"Well, it shouldn't be a problem for the shower! I wasn't planning on coming in for Christmas because I don't have enough vacation time to do both. You'll have to let me know when and where for the shower!"

"Okay, I will sweetie. Listen, I'm meeting Aubrey for dinner in a little while, so I need to go for now. Can I call you later with the details?"

"Of course...keep in touch and let me know something as soon as you can so that I can make arrangements with work and the airlines. Okay?"

"Okay, I'll call you soon. Bye Jackie...I love you!"

"I love you too Terri. Bye."

As I hung up the phone, a realization set in. Jackie obviously wasn't going to throw me a baby shower. But, at least she would be able to come into town for it. I missed seeing her. I missed talking to her about things, especially about Aubrey. I was anxious for them to meet and I knew Jackie would like her. No doubt in my mind...I know Aubrey will like her. We're like two peas in a pod and could've been twins

Well, the only thing I've got to do now is tell Aubrey Jackie won't be able to throw me the baby shower. If she could have, I felt like she would have brought it up in the conversation. Besides, how would she be able to being out of state and not having the vacation time? It didn't matter. I just wanted to see her. I'll just talk to Aubrey tonight about it and hopefully we will be able to make some sort of decision. The sooner we decide, the sooner Jackie can make her flight arrangements.

~

Reading her directions was like trying to read chicken scratch! I kept driving down the back roads from the lake, when I finally saw a sign that looked faintly familiar...Summer Field Estates. Slowly, I pulled into the subdivision. I kept driving, looking aimlessly at houses on both sides of the street, hoping to see one that looked a little familiar. This residential section was beautiful in all aspects. Even the streets were kept neat. In front of each house, the bold, black lettering of address numbers were neatly painted on the curb. It made it easy for persons like myself who were searching for a specific address. I kept searching for the numbers, 422. I remembered the neighborhoods for their immaculate lawns and flower gardens. Things were starting to come back to me about

162

that night. Searching for the right numbers, I glanced over to the right and just happen to see the exact address, 422. I came to an abrupt stop and stared up at the house. About that time, I saw a familiar face standing in the front entrance of her doorway. Aubrey and she was holding a cat...it must be Jasper. I wheeled into the driveway and parked in front of the garage door. This looked a little familiar, too. I put on the emergency break, opened the car door and got out.

"Recognize anything?" She was still standing at her front entrance doorway.

"Maybe a little...it's all still fuzzy I'm afraid."

I walked up the sidewalk and into the house through her front door, where I was greeted by Jasper. He was wrapping himself around my legs as if to say, welcome back, I've missed you. He was purring so loudly, I could hear him without getting down to his level. He continued to walk through and around my legs, rubbing his chin and whiskers on me as if I were a human scratching post. I leaned down to pick him up and he began to lick my face. Purring even louder than before, I laughed out loud and caught a glimpse of Aubrey. She was still standing in the doorway, arms folded across her chest and smiling, as she watched me with him.

"He is so wonderful! Why did you name him Jasper?"

"Actually, I wasn't the one who named him. I got him from the animal shelter. It was love at first sight. He was only about six months old when I brought him home."

I put him down and began to look around, hoping to recognize something. I was beginning to feel somewhat uncomfortable. It's like having amnesia, because I had obviously been here, but nothing I saw was familiar.

"Want a second tour to jog your memory?"

I looked over at her and nodded. She could sense I wasn't remembering anything, but I hoped she wouldn't see how tense I was feeling. She walked over to me, put her arms around me and held me for a moment. I could feel her heart beating against my chest. Still holding me, she pulled back slightly and looked at me.

"It's okay if you don't remember anything at all. When you hit your head, it knocked you out. Normally, people won't remember, even if they're knocked out even for a few seconds. So, don't worry about it. It will be okay. By the way, this where you fell and hit your head."

Pointing down to the floor, I could see where I had fallen.

"Really? Right here?"

"Yeah, right here."

By this time, Jasper was making a figure eight around our legs, weaving in and out like a race car driver.

"I think he likes you!"

She smiled and reached down to pick him up and held him in one arm and then, reached out to take my hand with the other. She closed my hand in hers and we started walking through different rooms in the house. Walking throughout each room, as before, was like I'd never seen anything as beautiful. I was glad she was giving me another tour. We finally finished the second tour by ending up back where we began. I watched her as she continued to cook our dinner in the kitchen. Jasper was following her around, hoping to find a morsel of food she might accidentally drop. They were made for each other, I thought. He was obviously her baby and anyone could tell she pampered him. She turned around and gestured for me to follow her out on the patio, where she had prepared a table for two.

The table was set much like mine except it wasn't sitting beside an in-ground pool. Dusk was setting in and the illumination of the lights in the pool made me feel I was somewhere in the Caribbean. Even though it's been a warm week, It's hard to believe Christmas is right around the corner. Whatever cold spell we had earlier, it was long gone by now.

"How about a swim after dinner?"

"You're kidding, right?"

"No, I'm serious! Besides, the pool's heated."

"Well, I don't have a bathing suit with me..."

"Well, I've got a suit I think you'll have no problems wearing. Or, if you'd rather not wear one, that will be okay too."

I watched her face light up as she smiled at me. That same beautiful smile I love to see.

"Uh, I'll try the suit..." I smiled back at her and we both walked back into the house where she led me upstairs to her bedroom. She opened the dresser, where she pulled out a bathing suit for me to try on. She laid it on the bed and then turned and left, closing the door behind her. I took the suit into her master bath and stripped. For the first time, I saw how big my belly looked in a full-length mirror. Wow...I can't believe how big I was getting. I was only four months along and I'm already this big? My God, how much bigger am I going to get? Was she sure I wasn't having twins? Suddenly, I was feeling very unattractive. There was no way I was getting in that pool with or without this suit on!

"Are you okay in there?"

Aubrey was knocking on the bedroom door. I guess she thought I would be downstairs by now. Thank God I decided to go into the master bath.

"Uh...listen, I don't think this suit is going to work. Actually, I've gotten bigger than I thought. In fact, I look horrible..."

Now, there was a knock on the master bath door. Oh God, I don't want her to see me this way!

"Can I come in for a minute?" I didn't say anything for minute and then I figured if I didn't say something, she would come in anyway. Hell, I was in her bathroom!

"Well, I just didn't think I was this big yet. Are you sure I'm not having twins?"

"Terri, can I come in for a minute?" I opened the door and she walked in to find me half-naked, standing in front of the floor-length mirror with my big belly sticking out. She walked up behind me and placed her arms around my belly. She held me close. Then, she placed her hands on my belly and started rubbing in a circular motion. From behind, I could feel her pressed up against me. My breasts were swollen and felt as if they were sagging down to the ground. I watched her in the mirror as she continued to rub my belly. She looked as though she were enjoying herself. I just don't understand how she could find me attractive...especially now. She unwrapped her arms from behind and stood in front of me.

"Terri...yes, you are pregnant. But, not only are you pregnant but you are also beautiful. Your body is carrying a tiny human being and that's transforming into a baby. No matter what your body transforms into...you will still be the same person to me. You will still be as beautiful as the first day I saw you walk into my office. It's okay that your body is changing. I still think you are incredibly attractive. If you feel too uncomfortable about swimming in the pool tonight, we don't have to."

I continued to look at her and I could see it in her eyes. I could see how genuinely concerned she was feeling for me. She was right. There was nothing I could do at the moment, but be pregnant. Besides, this was what I had wanted for so long. I really needed to change my outlook on the way I had progressed with my pregnancy...and my body. Embarrassed by my selfish and negative thoughts, I finally conceded that I had to let this image go.

"Aubrey, thank you. Uh, why don't you give me a moment while I get into this suit and I'll meet you downstairs."

She turned to leave and then stopped. Turning back around, she stood in front of me once more and leaned in to kiss me. I closed my eyes and let her take me away for a moment. I wrapped my arms around her and kissed her passionately. I felt her sigh softly and my heart skipped a beat. I held her close and dared to dream where this passion was going. I couldn't believe how good she made me feel even with just a kiss. We were obviously passionate about one another. I loved kissing her. It was like a scene out of a movie where passion would take you to another level you were afraid to challenge.

I had never been so open with anyone, not even Annie. Aubrey just makes it easy to feel comfortable with her.

"I'll meet you downstairs when you're ready." She gave me a quick peck on the lips, shut the door to her bathroom, and left me standing once again in front of the full-length mirror.

"Okay, I'll be down in a minute."

I put on the suit and stared in the mirror once more. It would only get worse, I thought. I was only going to get bigger the further along I progressed in my pregnancy. I'd better get use to it. I put my clothes on over the suit and went back downstairs to where I found her waiting for me out on the patio.

"Are you okay?" She was sitting at the table she had prepared for us for dinner.

"Yes, I think I'll be okay after I get use to the idea of my weight. Besides, I know it's only going to get worse. I just look so disfigured! Don't you think?"

"Not at all Terri...you look beautiful pregnant. In fact, I remember when you came into my office and told me you had made the decision to have a baby. I remember thinking then how beautiful you would look pregnant. Listen, I've seen quite a few pregnant women in my clinic and there's no doubt in my mind that you are the most...."

"Oh Aubrey, stop...I know you're just trying to make me feel better. Listen, don't get me wrong, I appreciate what you're trying to do. It's just that...it's going to take a little bit of time for me to adjust to me looking like this."

God, I wish I had a glass of white zinfandel right now. Aubrey reached across the table and took my hand in hers. She had that look in her eyes. I could always tell when she was serious. I remember it from my surgery.

"Terri, how can I convince you?"

"You can't Aubrey...at least not now. I'll have to work through this. I've always been the thin one in my family. Five foot, four, blonde hair, blue eyes, and 115 pounds. Now look at me. Not any where close to that. Do you understand what I mean?"

"Yes, I do. As your doctor I can tell you that you are not overweight. You are exactly where you should be weight-wise."

"Well, yes as my doctor. But as my..."

"What? What were you going to say? As your what?" She was starting to smile by now.

Now she had caught me off-guard. I'm not sure what to say.

"I'm not sure...what are you? My partner, lover, friend? How would you describe yourself to me or what am I to you?"

At that point, I wasn't sure I was ready for what I was about to hear. Better now than later, I thought.

"Terri, I'm not sure either. All I can tell you is that I'm your doctor first. After that, I guess that's something we both need to figure out, isn't it? While you're thinking on that, why don't I serve us some dinner? Besides, we don't want you to hit the floor again, do we?"

It was almost eight o'clock by now and we had pretty much lost all track of time.

"You're right about that. What are we having for dinner anyway?"

"It's a surprise! I'm bringing it out in a second."

I watched her walk toward the kitchen. What a great looking body she had. She had on a pair of faded blue jeans and a long-sleeve, mock turtleneck shirt. She had the sleeves pulled up almost to her elbows. If she had on a swimsuit underneath that, I couldn't tell! She quickly returned with a bowl full of salad, chicken breasts, baked potatoes and bread. What a feast! She served me first and then herself. We sat in silence for a minute as we ate. I thought for a moment...what would you call 'us'? I mean, we have been dating for a few months now and we've even slept together...once. We definitely have a connection. We seem to agree on most everything. So, where is this relationship going? What is the next step for 'us'? All I ever think about is her and this baby.

"Aubrey?"

I put down my fork and looked at her. She looked up at me and her eyes were searching mine. I could feel my heart pounding in my chest. I wasn't sure what I was going to say, but I had no time to rehearse. I didn't want to lose this special moment we had between us.

"Aubrey...what I want to tell you is this...I feel a special bond between us and we definitely have a connection. More than anything, I have never wanted someone as much as I do you. You make me feel special, not just as my doctor, but my other half. I feel you are so much a part of my life now and I don't want to lose that or you. All I think about is you...and this baby. I want you to be a part of its life and mine. I want us to be a family, together. When I go to bed at night I think of you and wonder if you are feeling the same. I want to hold you before you fall asleep at night. I want you lying beside me when I wake up in the mornings. My life has changed so much since you have come into my life. It's changed for the better. I'm more focused, I know what I want out of life, and it's all because of you and this baby. Without you, this baby would not have been possible. I feel with everything inside of me that you were sent to me for a reason. For whatever reason, I don't know. All I do know is that you make me very happy. I'm not sure what the next step is for 'us', but whatever it is, I'm sure it will only get better. Whatever rough spots come along, we'll get through it together. All I ask is that you be honest and up front with me. If this is not what you want, tell me now. Please, just tell me now. I don't want anyone else...I don't want to date anyone else, either. You are the one Aubrey. I just can't imagine spending my life with anyone else but you. I am so in-love with you. You have my heart and my soul lady. I am yours, if you'll have me."

I watched her for a moment as she searched my eyes. I could tell she wasn't expecting what I just told her. Now I was afraid. I wasn't sure what she was going to say...maybe I had said too much, too soon. I sat and waited in silence. She laid her fork down, took a drink of her wine and set the glass down.

"Do you know how long I have waited for you to say that to me? I had envisioned this conversation long ago before you even came into my office. You see, the *first* time I met you, I fell in-love with you. I know you don't remember me, because it's been such a long time ago when we met. We were at a party for a mutual friend...except, I was with Katie at the time. This was long before you left to go to Ohio. You came to the party with friends of yours from college and she introduced us. Anyway, I knew you weren't with anyone. I kept watching you walk around with your friends and I wanted so badly to come over and talk to you, but Katie was her usual self, drunk, and I felt the need to take care of her. Anyway, the party was over near Emory. I remember because you were so happy that classes were out and you were about to graduate. You all were celebrating your completion of years of hard work. Katie and I even came to graduation on that Saturday. I was hoping to run into you, but never did. I walked around in a daze for a while after meeting you, but then resumed back into the life with Katie. I knew after meeting you that night that I was not happy with her and it wasn't long afterwards that I left her. I would never imagine that years later you would return back into my life. I hoped one day that I would see you again and I hoped, in my time, I would somehow find you. But I never imagined it would be like this. So, you see, we have come full-circle. You have come back into my life...this time with dreams, passions, and even romance for me. What more could I even ask for? You have already started to share your life with me and you don't even know it. When I reflect back on those days, I wondered if I would ever be happy again. The only way I knew I would ever be happy, would be with you. You touched my soul that night I met you. You opened my eyes to a whole other world. I forgot what I was missing. I was settling for something and someone I didn't need or want in my life. All I had to do was let her go...in hopes I would find you. I finally did find you, even if it was several years later. You are my soul mate Terri. I found you not only once, but *twice*. I'm not about to let you go again! So, to answer your question...yes, I'll have you. I'm not letting you go. I'll be whatever you need me to be...your doctor, partner, wife...whatever you want, you have it. For as long as you'll have me, I'm yours. I would marry you tomorrow, if that's what you wanted."

I got up from the table, walked over in front of her and stood there for a moment staring at her in awe. I looked down at her and then bent down to hug her when she stood up and placed her arms around me. We stood there and hugged for what seemed like an hour. I held her close and stroked her hair, while she laid her head on my shoulder. I felt like we were silently dancing by the poolside. We were gently swaying to something... Maybe it was the music in our own heads. Even the water in the pool seemed to be swaying. The lights in the pool were just bright enough to see the gentle, wave-like motions of the water. How awesome was this? I can't imagine anything better. She lifted her head and looked at me for a moment and then I leaned in to kiss her. Her lips were so soft and gentle. She always took me to another place when we kissed. Somewhere I never wanted to leave. If it wasn't heaven, I don't know where else that it could be.

It was getting harder, leaving her, each time we spent together. I wondered how long it would be before we took the next step in our relationship. We were definitely a couple now. She was someone I would feel special locked arms with walking down the street in broad daylight. I wouldn't care what anyone said! She was just that special. We finally stopped swaying to the unheard music and just stood and looked at one another.

"Are you ready to take a swim with me?"

"Yes ma'am, I am."

I reached over and unbuttoned her jeans and then unzipped them. Slowly, I untucked her shirt from her jeans. She held her arms up high over her head and I pulled off her shirt. She had a bathing suit top on that accented her breasts beautifully. I helped her out of her jeans and saw how well her bikini bottoms fit her. She had a beautiful body and it made me ache for her. She started unbuttoning my shirt and soon it fell to the patio floor. I walked over to the table, sat down, and slid out of my pants. We took each other's hand and walked to the edge of the pool. She jumped into the shallow end, feet first, and then came back to the edge to help me in.

The chill of the air was just enough to make goose bumps stand up on every inch of your body, but the water was warm enough that it helped contain them. Standing in only three to four feet of water, I leaned up against the wall of the pool and watched her as she swam from one end to the other and then back to me. She had very graceful strokes. She swam over to me, put her arms around me and kissed me. The feel of her wet body excited me to no end. Her breasts were firm and nipples hard. I could see their firmness through her bathing suit top. She watched me as I unhooked her top and pulled it off slowly, exposing her firm breasts. Reaching down to her breast, I could feel her hand placed behind my neck. I stroked her nipple with my tongue and I felt her press my head hard into her body. I could hear her soft sighs and whispers. I pulled her closer in to me and held her from behind. As I slipped my hand underneath her bathing suit bottom, I felt her tremble and then her hand met mine. She was wetter than water. She kept me there until I heard her soft whispers for me to take her. Keeping me inside of her, she let it go with such force that she shook from exhaustion. I held her close to me until she regained composure. I thought how wonderful this feeling would be if it never ended.

V.A. Buck

Chapter 21

Getting up the next morning, I found her beside me, asleep in her bed. Quietly, I slid out of bed, headed to the bathroom and closed the door so I wouldn't disturb her. I was still amazed about our conversations we had during dinner last night. I had no idea she felt like that about me for so long. She was right, I didn't remember meeting her at that party. It didn't matter anyway because now we were together and that's all that mattered. We were well on our way to becoming a family. I felt like I could tell the entire world how happy I was that she and I were together.

Coming out of the bathroom and back into the bedroom, I could see she was still, sound asleep. I headed downstairs and into the kitchen. Jasper was eating his breakfast when he spotted me coming down the stairs. He met me at the bottom stair and began purring as he rubbed around my legs. I picked him up and held him close, scratching him behind his ears and under his chin. He sounded just like a motor boat. Carrying him through the kitchen, I went out through the patio doors and sat down at the table by the pool. Jasper sat on my lap and started to kneed. I thought about last night and tried to recap our night we had together. I didn't want to forget a single word of our conversations. But more than anything, I wanted to remember last night because It marked the beginning of our relationship. I felt like I would remember it forever. I even remember the beginning of my relationship with Annie...but that didn't matter anymore because now, I am happy and in-love with Aubrey.

"What could you possibly be thinking about this morning?" She had come up behind me and discovered I was in deep thought. Jasper, on the other hand, was snoozing in my lap, comfortably. She wrapped her arms around me and placed her cheek against mine.

"Oh, I think you know exactly what I was thinking about...you, of course." She came around and sat at the table with me.

"Want some hot tea this morning?"

"Only if you are going to have some with me."

She got up, kissed me on the cheek and went into the kitchen. Jasper jumped down and followed her. She returned after a few minutes, bringing us buttered toast and hot tea. Jasper was hot on her heels, trying desperately to keep up with the pace Aubrey had set. We ate our toast and sipped our hot tea, while reminiscing about our night together.

"I think I have an appointment with you that's coming up soon, don't I? Maybe you'll be able to tell what the sex of this child will be. In fact, the way I'm growing, maybe you'll see two of them instead of just one this time. You know, I love it when you examine me...you make me feel safe about this pregnancy. You're very positive and have a great bedside manner ma'am."

"To be honest, it is possible you could be pregnant with two and we just can't see it yet. I've known cases where both babies were conjoined, meaning they shared one body and had one heartbeat. I'm not saying this to scare you...but I've also seen a case or two where one baby is behind the other and can't be seen until the very end. So, we may not know anything until the day you deliver. I've seen stranger things."

"Well, for some reason, I'm not worried about this baby. I know I'm in good hands as long as you're my doctor. And by the way, thank you for being my doctor. I couldn't have done this without you. Do you know that? I guess I can officially say...you got me pregnant!"

"As your partner, nothing would please me more to know you were having my child."

~

Driving home from her house and remembering my appointment with her, I knew I would have to seriously start preparing the house for this baby. It's Christmas and I don't have much time to get prepared. I had been talking about this for weeks now, but I would have to make the commitment to do it... I needed to talk to Jackie. I'd better call her when I get in. I also needed to call Dad about some possible renovations. He would know what I needed. Besides, maybe he already knew what I was thinking...he was good at that kind of thing. Sometimes, he just seemed to know what needed to be done before anyone said anything. I think he has a sixth sense or something. Nevertheless, I had to get on the ball and get this accomplished...in fact, I better be thinking of two instead of one, just in case. With my luck, I'll have *twins*. I'd better call Dad first, then Jackie.

"Dad, is that you? What are you doing?" I could hear some background noise.

"Oh, hi Terri...hold on and let me turn down this Christmas special."

I waited for a second and then I could hear the noise dissipate in the background.

"Listen Dad, the reason I'm calling is because I'm a little worried I may not have enough room for the baby when it comes. What do you think about making some renovations out here?"

"Terri, I have already thought about it and if you want, I can bring out some plans for you to look at. What do you think?"

"I figured you might be thinking along the same lines...can you come out today for a little while?"

"Sure, I can come now if you like? Will you be home for a little while?"

"Sure Dad, come on...I'll fix us some lunch, unless you've already eaten."

"That's fine. I'll be on in a few minutes. Do you want your mother to come too?"

"Of course, I have some things to discuss with her anyway."

We agreed to meet and I was excited to see the plans he devised. I'm glad he had thought ahead... I went ahead and made sandwiches and ice tea for all of us when I saw his car pull up in the driveway.

"Hi mom. How have you been feeling lately? Is your medicine working any better?" I could see where her eyes were focused...on my belly.

"Hi honey...yes, I've been feeling okay for now. More importantly, how are you feeling?"

"Well, as you can see...I'm getting bigger by the moment. My doctor still says she only hears one heartbeat, but I swear I have this funny feeling I'm having twins for some reason. Look at me! I'm huge!"

"Honey, you just feel like that because you're use to being thin all of your life. It's perfectly natural for you to be putting on a few pounds and expanding at the waistline.

Don't worry, you've got an excellent doctor and she will take good care of you."

If she only knew, I thought...if she only knew. Dad brought out the plans and showed me what he considered as renovations. I had something more in mind. I actually took him to the spot where I thought could be expanded and divided into some more room. He shook his head and gave me reasons why it couldn't be done. I brought out the big gun...the biggest renovation of all, which was to put a second story addition on top of the house. He just looked at me.

"Do you have any idea how much..."

"Dad, I don't care...I'll mortgage if I have to. This baby and I will have to have more room. Otherwise, I'll need to move."

I had no intentions of moving, but he didn't know that. It was my way of getting him to understand how serious I was about making the necessary and much needed renovations for my new baby and me...or babies. For now, a new baby was enough for me to think about. Dad said he would have to think about a major construction project like this and get back with me. It didn't matter what he thought by this time. I would have to do something soon, regardless of cost. He took a few measurements as mom and I sat and chatted about clothes and baby furniture and other baby stuff. When he had completed his list of measurements, they were off to run some errands. Now, I had to call Jackie. I had to fill her in on all that had been happening with Aubrey and me. Maybe she had some insight to this room dilemma. I was about to pick up the phone to call her when the phone rang.

"Hello?" For a second or so, there was no one there. I had an eerie feeling come over me as if I shouldn't have answered the phone. Suddenly, I heard a familiar voice on the other end of the line.

"Terri?"

My stomach sank and my chest nearly collapsed. It was Annie.

"Annie? Is that you? Where are you?"

"I'm...I'm calling from Ohio. How are you? I haven't heard from you in quite some time. I thought I would give you a call to see how things are going with you."

"Annie, you told me you wanted no contact with me. I was just abiding by your wishes, that's all. I'm fine, actually. How are you doing?"

"Well, the reason I'm actually calling is...is because I would like to talk to you about something."

I had the distinct feeling something was very, very wrong. I could always tell when she had something on her mind. This didn't sound good.

"What do you want to discuss Annie?"

"Us."

I nearly fell out on to the floor from shock. Never in my wildest dreams would I ever imagine she would want to discuss 'us'.

"Us? What about us?"

"Well, that's what I wanted to talk to you about... I thought maybe we could start over?"

I could feel my lunch starting to rise up into my throat, as if I would be sick. I had found the love of my life and there was no way I could ever go back to her. I loved her for ten years. Oh God, that seemed like so long ago. Actually, it had only been about a year since I came home. Now, she was calling, wanting to get back together. I still loved her, but not in-love with her. Not like I am with Aubrey, I thought.

"Annie, why now? Why are you calling me now?"

"I feel as though I made a terrible mistake by letting you go...I'm sorry. I was going through so much at the time and I suppose if the truth were known, I thought I didn't love you anymore. But, I was wrong. I do still love you. I still want you in my life."

"Oh God, Annie. There's so much that's happened since I've been home."

"You've met someone, haven't you?"

"Annie, I'm sorry...yes, I have met someone. And that's not all."

"What do you mean by that?"

"Well, when I came home last March, all I could think about was you. All I could think about were the dreams I had about us and what we both wanted. Living by myself made me realize that just because you weren't in my life any longer didn't mean I had to give up my dreams. So, I have pursued them, one by one. I'm happy to say that I have fulfilled many of them. What I need to tell you is this...I'm going to be a mother in June."

There was silence on the other end of the line for what seemed like an eternity. I could tell this news was not something she had expected to hear. She knew I loved her with everything inside of me, and when I left that cold day in March, she knew my spirit was killed. I lost my soul that day, but she thought she was doing the right thing. I guess she thought I would go back to her without question. She never expected that I would find someone else, especially this soon.

"Annie, are you still there?"

"Yes, I'm still here. I'm just...I'm just taking it all in I guess. I never thought you would go through with it. I mean, I guess I didn't think you were serious about having a child. But, I'm happy for you, if this is what you really want. Are you having the baby together with this person you're with..."

I didn't expect that question to come out of her mouth. I don't know why I didn't expect it. It really shouldn't surprise me because she was never subtle about questions or discussions. She was someone who didn't like to beat around the bush, so to speak.

"Annie, as of this minute, no. But, after the baby is born, we will raise it together. I have changed a lot since I've come home. You can't imagine the turmoil I went through leaving you behind after ten years. I knew I didn't want to go through that again. In fact, I didn't intend to meet someone else. It just happened, when I least expected it. I had intended to spend the rest of my life alone. I knew my heart would never be able to go through another loss. That's why I wanted to have this child. He would love me unconditionally. I wanted to share the rest of my life with someone who would love me no matter who or what I was to him. I had everything I ever needed. All the materialistic things in my life were complete, Annie. I just needed someone to share my life. That was something you didn't want to do. Now, not only am I going to have a child but also have someone special in my life to share my child and be a family. Not only do I feel complete, but also I feel blessed. You see, there was a possibility that I couldn't have children because of my age and my family history. I am now four and going on five months pregnant. My family is ecstatic about the whole thing. They can't wait for a grandchild...maybe even twins."

"Twins?"

"It's a good possibility...i had an awesome donor. But, it's too soon to tell at the moment."

"Terri, I don't know what to say...I just never expected this."

I could tell her feelings were hurt because I was not going to discuss getting back together with her. I had finally come to terms with myself that it was over between us. I wasn't sure how I felt about that realization. But, to tell the truth, I hadn't thought about her since I had been involved with Aubrey. I knew that was a good sign. She would get over it and move on with her life eventually. Now she knew how I felt after all these months.

"Annie, I'm sorry. My life is finally coming together and I am happy. I'm sorry I had to put you through this, but I thought you deserved the truth."

"I appreciate you being honest with me. I'm not going to say that I'm fine with all of this, because I can't. I'm not fine with it...but I'll get use to it. That's all I can say for now."

"You will meet someone Annie. When you least expect it, you'll meet the right one."

I never thought I would ever be saying that to her...not in a million years. We said our good-byes and I hung up the phone. I sat on the couch and stared into space for a long time. I couldn't believe she had called and I couldn't believe she had asked me to come back to her. More than anything else, I couldn't believe I said no. Somehow I feel relieved, yet guilty at the same time. I started to cry uncontrollably. Oh God, where was Aubrey when I needed her?

V.A. Buck

Chapter 22

Trying to find something to wear to my doctor's appointment always seemed like a chore. I never knew what I was going to wear because I never knew what was going to fit right. I hated anything that was binding around my stomach. Fumbling through my closet, I stumbled across a shirt I'd never seen, or at least I didn't remember buying one like this. It looked like something I would buy though. Aubrey and I had purchased so many clothes at that second hand store that it wouldn't surprise me if I didn't remember it. I took it out and decided I would wear it today.

Getting ready this morning was difficult, especially after last night's conversation with Annie. I felt almost depressed this morning. Just hearing her voice was enough to send me back ten years without even trying. I didn't want to go back...not even ten years. What we had was long ago and it was something we shared. But, it was time to move on and I knew that after having that conversation with her.

I was with someone else now and I liked the idea of getting ready to start a family with her. I needed her to hold me last night. I needed to talk to her about this. I wanted to call Aubrey so badly last night, but I felt the conversation I had with Annie should be discussed in person. I had to tell her...in fact, I wanted to tell her. I didn't want to keep anything from her because I felt she needed to know. If the moment were right today, I would bring up the conversation during my appointment. If it wasn't, maybe we could discuss it tonight after she got off work. I couldn't think about it now or I knew I would get upset again.

I finished dressing and set out to keep my appointment with Aubrey. I was eager for this appointment anyway. I hoped today, like every appointment, that I would learn what sex my child would be or if I were having more than one. Maybe today would be the day. Besides, I needed some good news after last night.

Driving down the same route to her office, I tried to think of pleasant things. Something that would keep me feeling positive and blessed of so many wonderful things that are happening in my life right now. I just had to think of Aubrey and a smile would automatically show up on my face. She truly made me happy in all areas of my life. She was my anchor, the missing piece of the puzzle and soul mate. Without her, I knew I wouldn't be this happy. Of course, I guess no one is truly happy without love in their life. I felt lucky in love, I guess. More than that...I felt we were meant to be.

In my lifetime, I never thought I would find the right one. Then, Annie came along. I always thought Annie was the one, but when she let me go, it was obvious she wasn't. Now, I have Aubrey. From age, experience, wisdom and grief comes maturity. It's like an inner maturity. I don't know how else to explain what I was feeling. I'm not sure if it's the pregnancy or a combination of events that have been happening to me. All I knew was that I was in-love and I couldn't wait to share my life and child with her. I was ready to be a family and I wanted to share everything with her. If I could give her the moon and the stars, I would...on a solid gold platter. I want her to know everyday how much I love her. I don't want her to have any reservations, or be hesitant about being my partner. If there were anything about me or us she was unsure about, I would want her to question it or approach me about it. I thought my life would change when I became pregnant, but I had no idea how much I would change when I met her. She was everything I had ever wanted.

Driving up the driveway to her office, I felt somewhat better. I couldn't wait to see her. Sometimes, just to be near her was enough. It just felt right, safe, balanced, and like a sweet dream. I loved my sweet dreams with her.

"Terri are you ready to come on back?" I followed her down the hall once again to the exam room, where I put on the gown and sat on the exam table until she arrived. Those exam tables were always so cold.

"Hey Terri, how are you feeling?"

"Hi Aubrey, I'm feeling pretty good.

She began to examine my belly and me and then began listening to the heartbeat. I watched her as she listened intently to the baby's heartbeat. I knew she was trying to hear another one. I gave her time to conduct the examination and then felt okay enough to proceed with the conversation about Annie.

Listen, I need to talk to you about something that happened to me last night. I actually started to call you, but I wanted to tell you in person. Guess who called me last night?"

"I have no idea, tell me."

"Annie called me."

"Annie?"

"Yes, Annie...she called to see how I was doing and to..."

"Ask you to come back to her?"

"How did you know?" I could tell she was getting really uncomfortable about this conversation. She wouldn't even look at me.

"Listen, Aubrey, I told her that I had met someone really wonderful and I was very happy. I told her I was sorry if I hurt her feelings, but I felt she deserved the truth. I also told her that my life was finally coming together by having a baby and a family. I even told her my own family was ecstatic about the baby. I basically told her everything...I was blatantly honest with her."

I noticed she was busy conducting the ultrasound.

As she continued watching the monitor, she had her back to me as I divulged the truth. When I finished telling her my side of the story, she turned around and faced me.

"Really? You told her everything? Even about us being a family?" I could tell she was relieved.

"I promise, I told her everything. Yes, even about us becoming a family. There's no way in hell I would go back to her Aubrey...no way. You make my life complete."

"I am relieved to know you wouldn't go back to Ohio. I know I shouldn't feel this insecurity about us, but for once in my life, I feel that I have met the right woman for me. I don't want to lose you to anyone. I lost so much in my life when I was with Katie...I suppose that's where this insecurity stems from. With Katie, I never knew from one minute to the next how my life was going to go during the day. I had to literally live one minute at a time with her, and I don't want to do that anymore with anyone else. I want to be able to feel that I can trust you. Actually, if the truth were known, I feel I can trust you. That's a huge step for me with someone new. If I didn't, I wouldn't have become involved with you. I couldn't predict what you would've done, but I was scared that 'if' Annie called...oh God, what if you did go back to her. I have to tell you...I was more scared about that than I even care to admit to myself. Now that I know for sure, I can tell you I am relieved that you aren't going back to Ohio. I do have to ask you a question about your conversation with her, though."

"What is it?"

"Was it hard for you to tell her no?"

"I have to tell you, Aubrey, I was so shocked that she even called I didn't give her or our past another thought. I just said no...because you came to mind so quickly. I didn't hesitate, beat around the bush or hem-haw around. I just politely said, no. Besides, I am not in-love with her anymore...I am in-love with YOU! You have my heart and soul, not her."

It wasn't long after that exam when we decided we would live together after the baby was born. This was yet another new chapter in my life and I was both excited and nervous about our decision.

~

It was Christmas present to myself and to my child to begin renovations on the house. It was time for dad to start the baby's room first on the second story, and then complete the rest of the addition afterwards. Living by the water was my serenity and I didn't want to give up that part of my soul. Besides, Aubrey liked it here and I knew she would be happy no matter where we lived.

I contacted dad about the renovation decisions and he soon arrived to go over the plans. I basically told him everything I wanted, how I wanted it done, and to my amazement, he agreed. I left the contracting to him but gave him a budget and a deadline. His eyebrows raised and then he conceded. I realized I had put him in an awkward position to push this project hard. But I had faith he would be able to complete it on time. He knew I was getting close to my due date and I think that was all it took for him. The next few weeks would try my patients to the limit, but I knew it would be worth it in the long run. My baby would have his own room, plus, we would have enough room for Aubrey. Finally, a family of my own.

Aubrey and I decided to spend some quality time alone during Christmas. We also decided to exchange gifts, but set a monetary limit. We frequented each other's homes and then were able to spend some time with mom and dad. Her family was unable to come down from Boston this year. I could tell she was somewhat disappointed, but that soon dissipated once she joined us for the typical southern Christmas dinner. She was amazed at the feast mother was able to cook. All the fixings, trimmings, vegetables, desserts, and of course the huge turkey. We were stuffed to the point where no one wanted any dessert for awhile! We helped mother clean up the kitchen and then we left. I was exhausted and I know Aubrey was tired. For the day after Christmas, she had an early start with surgery scheduled at seven a.m. We called it a night. This had been one of the best Christmases I can ever remember. My whole family was happy over something as simple as a baby. Isn't it amazing how a baby can make you feel?

~

Now that Christmas was over and the New Year had begun, it was time to get the ball rolling. The next few days turned into weeks. By now, spring wasn't far off and any chance to get ahead in the renovations was a plus, especially to try and stay ahead of any bad weather. The construction crews frequented my driveway with vehicles filled with materials for the new rooms. Their task of putting a new level on an existing roof would prove to be challenging, but not impossible. Local home improvement warehouses were delivering new materials on a daily basis and I never knew what would be in my driveway next. First it was sheets and sheets of plywood and framing materials and then the drywall arrived. Hammers hitting nails and saws cutting wood were loud and annoying sounds. Dust had begun to settle everywhere in the house and I eventually gave up trying to clean up at the end of each day. Aubrey advised me to wear a dust mask until the construction was completed. It soon became a regular piece of clothing I put on every morning.

Nevertheless, the baby's room was coming together quickly and soon it would be finished. I would be able to start arranging the baby's furniture and other things, getting it ready in time for the birth. On one hand, I wished I had started this project earlier, but on the other hand, I was just glad that it was becoming a reality.

Weeks later, the major construction was finally completed and now the interior rooms had to be finished with all new electrical, plumbing, windows, doors, and fixtures. Specific colors of paint and carpeting had to be chosen. My patients were being tried on every level, but I had to maintain my civility. After all, they were doing what I asked of them. Their professional experience would show me the perfect, end result. I just wasn't use to the noises and strangers in my own house. I had to continue being flexible and tolerant.

Now in my third trimester, it was a constant struggle to show tolerance on any level. I was ready for the noise, dust, unfamiliar voices, and lack of privacy to end. The project was almost ready to reveal itself in the immaculate way my father knew I would approve. I trusted his judgment because he knew my expectations.

He knew I wouldn't settle for anything less than perfection. The workers were way ahead of schedule and I knew it would be completed soon. The baby shower had been planned, guests invited, and Jackie would be flying in soon to be a part of it all. I wanted to make sure everything was perfect.

I was growing tired, physically, and needed help. Aubrey was stopping by daily, making sure I was okay and then staying with me night after night to ease my highest levels of stress. I felt secure with her now and didn't want her anywhere else but by my side. No two people suited each other more. The bond between us was clearly growing stronger. I couldn't wait to start our life and family "together."

Chapter 23

Since my last exam, I forgot to ask Aubrey what, if anything, she had seen on the monitor. I wondered if the baby had revealed itself in a way where I would know which colors to paint the baby's room. I had been so engulfed in the conversation about Annie that I completely forgot about the results from my exam. How, I don't know. Most of our conversations were like that, though. Totally captivated by one another's thoughts . We seemed to know what the other would say and sometimes, even finish each other's sentences. We would be so amazed that we would even be thinking the same thing. Somehow, I knew we would grow old together. I just wished I remembered her from years ago because we could've started this relationship earlier and been spared the hardship of our ex's. I guess it just wasn't meant to be until now.

My relationship with Aubrey makes me appreciate the hard times with Annie. If I hadn't come home when I did, we might not have crossed paths again. I guess it was actually perfect timing. I've never felt so positive in my life and this relationship feels so good and so right. I finally feel connected somehow. Maybe it's our spirits that are connected. What a wonderful feeling this is to have a positive relationship with someone so smart, beautiful, and who also feels the connection. More than anything, I believe that my child will also feel a connection between the two of us. My life just seems to be getting better and better. I couldn't want for more, except for this child to be born.

~

I awoke from my nap and headed into the kitchen for a snack. Ice cream seems to always be the perfect cure for everything that ails you. Grabbing the biggest bowl I could find and the ice cream scoop, I began the quest for sheer pleasure! I scooped and scooped until I finally decided that three scoops of Heavenly Hash would satisfy my craving. I headed for the couch and along the way, grabbed the remote. It was time for Oprah.

Stopping me dead in my tracks, I felt the pain I had dreaded...the contractions were here. At an instant, my water broke and I fought hard to keep my emotions under control. Why now? The baby is early! I had to call Aubrey soon, because now that my water had broken, the baby was on the way. Dialing her cell number, I could feel the contractions were becoming very intense and seemed closer and closer together.

"Aubrey, hi it's me. My water has just broken and the contractions are becoming very intense. The baby is early! Please call me!"

I knew I didn't have much time to wait. I sat and tried to remain calm but the pain was getting worse and trying to breathe through the contractions was next to impossible. What am I going to do if she doesn't call soon? What was the back-up plan? I'm not sure if we had one, but now was a good time to remember! What seemed like hours, I decided to call mom for a ride to the hospital.

"Mom...it's time. The baby is coming too soon! My water has already broken and the contractions are progressing to a few minutes apart! Can you come pick me up and take me to the hospital?"

"Honey, we are on our way! Try and stay calm..."

Within minutes they arrived, grabbed my bag, put me in the front seat and dad sped off in a fury. Dialing Aubrey's cell number again, I left another message that mom had picked me up and we were on our way to the hospital. I wondered where she was and why she hadn't returned my calls. I thought for a moment and rationalized she was probably in surgery.

I tried not to watch the road as dad drove frantically in and out of traffic. This time of the day, in particular, was the toughest. He turned on the emergency flashers and I thought for an instant that if the police pulled him over, I would probably curse him to no avail.

"Dad, can't you go any faster!" I could just feel the anger and irritability brewing. I was losing my tolerance for just about everybody and everything by now. And if the truth be known, I was scared to death I was going to lose this baby. Especially, now that my water had broken. Where was Aubrey? Why hadn't she called me back by now? I know my cell phone is on...

"Look out!"

Out of the corner of my eye I saw something coming at us. As if occurring in slow motion, a car was coming right at us and was going to hit us on my side of the door. I could feel myself trying to brace for the impact, but it was too late. I closed my eyes and cringed as I felt the impact slam me into the door. I heard mother scream as glass, from the windshield, exploded all over us. The car felt like it was swerving back and forth out of control. Each hit yanked me continuously around the front seat of the car like a pinball. Dad tried to keep the car from hitting other vehicles in our path, but it was impossible. The echoing sounds of metal hitting against metal were almost deafening and after it seemed like one intense hit after another, the battered car finally came to a jerking halt. I was so dizzy with confusion that I just couldn't move. Lying still and hearing only silence, I fought every muscle to try and move, but it was hopeless. My baby...

Chapter 24

"Jackie, do you think you could stay awhile this time around? I mean, I think we really need your help on this one."

"Dad, of course I can stay for awhile. In fact, I have already contacted my work and told them what's happened. I can stay as long as you need me. I wonder when they will let her go home?"

"I don't know Jackie, but when they bring her in from surgery, let's not talk about it. I don't want her to hear anything we say right now. She might not actually be able to hear anything, but I don't want to take that chance. Okay? I just hope she will be okay. Damn it, I never meant for anything like this to happen! I don't even know how it happened! It all just happened so fast..."

"Dad, no one is blaming you and you certainly shouldn't be blaming yourself. It was an accident and not your fault. The police even said so! Not only that, but you have to understand something else. First of all, Terri would never blame you for this accident. Secondly, neither would mom. You were on a mission to get her to the hospital and that guy didn't have a clue what he was doing!"

"Shh... Here they come."

Everyone was silent while Aubrey helped the recovery team escort Terri to her hospital room. Terri lay motionless in the hospital bed with IV tubes running from her body to a cold, steel pole. No one was sure what the other was thinking when they brought Terri in the room, but anyone could tell it was a very quiet and somber moment. Most everyone was afraid to ask the obvious question…which was, what about the baby? Did the baby survive the ordeal and if so, what kind of shape was he or she in?

"Aubrey, is Terri going to be okay?"

"Jackie, they had to take the baby by cesarean because of the trauma. He is in the neonatal unit now being observed. They're doing assessments just to make sure he will be okay. Terri, on the other hand, is…well, she is going to have a hard time recovering."

"What do you mean?"

"Because the car hit on her side, she took most of the impact. The trauma from that caused some hemorrhaging to occur after the cesarean. Additional surgery had to be performed to stop the bleeding. Because of the massive hemorrhage, blood transfusions were given. She is going to be on several antibiotics, pain meds, and will need total care for the next few weeks. That means whenever she is allowed to go home, she will need help with the baby and herself as well. Right now, they are keeping her drugged because of the intense trauma she has endured. She will be asleep for at least the next twenty-four hours. We are all in for a very long and critical period. Especially, the next forty-eight hours. This will be the time to watch for infection to set in and cause additional problems. It is the most crucial period. I won't lie to you and try to sugar coat this…but it could go either way right now. But for now…she is stable."

Jackie looked over at dad and watched the blood drain from his face. What was written all over his face was hard for Jackie to accept. He sat motionless for a moment, staring ahead as if he was lost in thought. Then, finding the strength to say what was in his heart, he leaned forward looking straight into Aubrey's eyes.

"You mean, she could die?"

Without hesitation, Aubrey held strong in her demeanor and her tone. She had been holding on to the adrenaline that kept her from being emotional over Terri. She looked back at dad and straight into his eyes.

"Yes sir, your daughter could die. But, they are doing everything possible for her. Also, I checked on your wife while I was in the ER, and I believe she will be okay. The good news is that she has no broken bones, but she will be bruised and sore for awhile."

Time just seemed to stand still at that moment. Everyone in the room breathed a sigh of relief for mother and a sigh of disbelief for myself. I was glad mother would be okay after the horrible ordeal. Listening to Aubrey discuss my medical condition in front of everyone was strange. It was as if I wasn't there; but I was lying in the hospital bed just a few feet from where they stood. It just all seemed like a dream. I could tell Aubrey was worried. I could hear it in her voice.

"Why don't you all go home now and I will stay the night with her and monitor her condition. I will call if there is any change. Besides, your wife will need you tonight. Jackie, would you mind to go by Terri's and look after the cats before you go home?"

"No, not at all. Do you have a key? I don't think I have mine with me."

"Sure, I think my keys are here in my purse somewhere. Ah, here they are. If you want to bunk out there, I'm sure Terri wouldn't care. Whatever you want to do is fine with me. I wasn't sure if you had made plans to stay with someone here in town or not."

"Actually, I really didn't have time to make any plans. I just had enough time to find a plane to get on and I flew in. So, that's fine with me. I can bunk there for awhile and help out if you need me to or until other plans have been made. Besides, I'm sure the cats would like to have some company."

"Okay then, it's settled. I will stay with her tonight and the rest of you go home and get some rest. It has been a really stressful day for all of you. We can't do her any good unless we are rested ourselves. So, I'll see you all in the morning."

As my family left, I could hear the door close behind them. Aubrey walked closer and sat on the bed next to me. She gently took my hand and held it in hers. Her hands were soft and warm, but I could feel she was trembling. I knew she was afraid. She laid her head on my shoulder and I heard her let out a long sigh. It was as if she finally accepted everything that had just happened.

As I lay there, listening to her breathe, I realized I couldn't respond to her. Mentally, I was intact. I could hear everything that was happening around me. I just couldn't physically respond. I couldn't put my arms around her and hold her or tell her that everything would be okay. Although I didn't feel any pain, I couldn't decipher the difference between what was critical and what wasn't. But, I knew Aubrey was very aware of the critical issues. It was only a matter of time before the doctors would be bring me out of this controlled and drug-induced state that I was in. I, unfortunately, had to play the waiting game. All I could do was listen to what was being said so that I could try and keep up with what my body was doing. Isn't that strange, I thought? I have no clue what my body is doing. I have ultimately no control. That's a scary thought. At this point, all I know is that I was in a car wreck, I have a son that I haven't seen yet, and I've just had major surgery. This is the time in my life where I don't have a choice, but to trust. I have to trust that everyone knows what they're suppose to do. Aubrey finally fell asleep, so I just lay here listening to the night sounds of the hospital.

Nurses would come in every so often and check my IV. I could tell because of the slight pull on top of my hand where it had been inserted. At the foot of the bed, I could hear the sliding of the clipboard against the bed as they were removing my chart and probably recording vital signs. There were constant footsteps in and out of my room. Sometimes, I heard a whisper or two from a nurse, which indicated to me that more than one nurse was in the room. I couldn't have slept anyway, it was much too busy in my room to get any peace and quiet. I wondered how much longer I would have to lie here and wait.

I missed being in my own bed, or rather our bed, holding her. I missed listening to music just before I went to bed. It always relaxed me. If I had soothing music now to listen to, I knew it would put me to sleep. I was so tired and I really did want to get some rest. I just wanted my brain to settle down and stop going a thousand miles an hour. But more than anything, I wanted to wake up and see my son. Concentrating on relaxing, I felt myself drifting closer and closer toward sleep. Without a sound for what seemed like hours, I heard the door open with sounds of a crying baby. I wanted to say, "what's wrong?" But, before I could have uttered those words, Aubrey jumped out of bed and ran to the door.

V.A. Buck

Chapter 25

"I think he's hungry. Do you want to feed him or should I take him back to the nursery?"

It was my son! Oh, how I wanted to get out of this bed just to be able to see and hold him for the first time! But, I couldn't do either.

"No, I'll feed him. Hi there, little one. Your mama is too sick to feed you right now, so I hope I will do for the moment. We sure have been excited to see you. Look at you, you are absolutely the spitting image of your mama, and so handsome! Let's sit down here in the rocker and I'll feed you."

Whether Aubrey knew it or not, she was giving me a play-by-play action. I was glad she had taken control of the situation. I listened very intently to the way she was describing him. I'm sure she could have said a little more about him in detail, but nevertheless, I was just glad she had him in the room with us and was taking good care of him. I can't believe he looks like me. I would have thought he would have taken on the strong genes of this father. I wasn't complaining though...just curious as to what he really looks like. I'm sure I will see him soon enough. It sounded as if Aubrey had softened her tone and decided to whisper. I focused really hard on what she was telling him.

"You know, your mama hasn't told me your name, so I hope you won't mind me calling you, 'little one.' You have no idea what you have been through these past few hours. But one day, I'll fill you in when you're big enough. Your mama has waited a lifetime for you. Did you know that? I can't wait to see the look on her face when she finally gets to see and hold you for the first time. She will be as proud of you as I am...No, no she won't. She will be more."

As I continued to listen to her talk to him, I wondered how I would've made it this far had it not been for her love and devotion to me. I honestly had been given a gift when she walked into my life this past year. Without her, none of this would have been possible. If I were to look back on my life with Annie, I can see how selfish we had become...it was all about the material things. I suppose it's a hard lesson to learn, but I would rather see it for what it really was than rationalize what I wanted it to be. Maybe the Red-Tail Hawk had a purpose after all in nesting behind the cabin. It was her that gave me the insight and courage to follow my dream of having this baby. It was the insight that allowed me to seek the truth about myself. What an amazing experience this has been. It's as if I had lacked something special in my life until she came along. I really don't want to waste another minute lying here in this state, when I could be enjoying time with my new little family. That's what it's all about...that's what love is really about. As a friend once said, "don't ever leave a stone unturned..." Now, I know what she really meant.

~

"Good morning Jackie. Did you sleep okay?"

"Actually, I think I was exhausted! I don't even remember going to sleep. I woke up to purring cats all around me this morning. I think they were just glad to have the company. How did you sleep last night?"

"I don't believe I slept very well. The nurse brought the baby in last night and I decided I would go ahead and feed him...you know, for the bonding experience. Especially since she is not able to right now. I guess I was up about every three to four hours. Plus, I was so worried about her. The good news is that I think she is out of the critical stage."

"Hopefully, it won't be too much longer. On the other hand though, she will feel all the aches and pains when she wakes up. She's already been through so much...you just have no idea what she's been through, Aubrey. God, I just hate to see her in pain."

Aubrey dropped her head and looked away. How she hated hearing about Terri's pain. So undeserving, she thought. After a few seconds, she turned back around to look at Jackie.

"You meant Annie, didn't you?"

Jackie could feel her eyes becoming big as saucers and she held her breath for fear she might say something she might regret. Aubrey turned away, shaking her head as if she were disgusted. Not knowing what had been discussed between them, Jackie calmly approached Aubrey and waited for the right moment to speak.

"She told you about her?"

"Yes, finally. But, I also told her about my ex and what she put me through...so I would say we have exchanged war stories. Besides, I would rather it be that way...out in the open and not hiding anything from each other. It just makes it more of a trusting relationship."

"Listen, mom and dad will be here soon, so we won't be able to speak this freely in front of them. So, there's just one thing I want to say...I have never heard Terri so happy when she called me in Texas and told me all about you. I never thought she would ever get over Annie, until you came along. I knew then, she would have a chance at happiness. Now, not only does she have you, but also a new baby. She has always wanted a child, but more than that...I think she has always wanted a family of her own. Now she has one with you."

At that point, the door opened and both Aubrey and Jackie parted without another word. Aubrey went to Terri's bedside and Jackie went to sit down across from Terri's bed.

"Good morning Aubrey...how is my daughter doing this morning? Is she stable?"

Gaining her composure, Aubrey turned off her personal emotions about Terri and took on her professional demeanor as a doctor.

"Well, as far as I can tell, she looks to be out of the critical stage. Her vitals are stable, color is good, and I believe she rested well last night."

"How are you feeling Mrs. Carter? Were you able to get some rest last night after leaving the hospital?"

"I have to tell you, I was very glad the emergency room doctor gave me a prescription for pain medication. Without it, I don't think I would have been able to rest. Even my arthritis eased up some. That, in itself, was some relief. I am a little sore this morning, but I think I will be fine. Jackie, did you rest well?"

"Actually mom, I did. By the way, where's dad?"

"Well, since Terri is incapacitated, your father is over at her house trying to make some home décor decisions about wall colors and carpeting. Since your father is a little color blind, I think he will need some help. Anyway, that's all that's left to do with the project. So, he wanted to get that out of the way and finished by the time Terri and the baby got home from the hospital. Speaking of which, where is my grandson?"

"They should be bringing him in soon for a feeding. Would you like to do the honors?"

"Oh, of course I would!"

"Look, here he comes now... Here, why don't you sit in the rocker and I'll scoot out and let you have some family time with him. I've got to go home, take a shower and feed my cat before I go to work. Call me if there's any change, Jackie. You've got my cell number, right?"

"I don't think I do...let me check my purse. Better give it to me again, so that I won't lose it."

"Okay, it's 555-1510, got it?"

"Got it. I promise, I'll call if there's any change."

"Okay, I'll see you all later this evening. Now, if you need anything, let me know. I'll stop by Terri's to see if I can help with anything before I come back to the hospital. See you all later."

Aubrey left the room and let the door close behind her. She turned and peeked through the long, narrow window in the door at Terri. She was just lying there lifeless. She didn't think she could stand much more of being alone and without her. Frustrated and feeling helpless, she turned away and headed home.

"It's hard to imagine that either of you girls were this small...but, you were. I wonder how much he weighs? I bet he doesn't weigh an ounce over seven pounds. Jackie, he looks exactly like Terri when she was born! I wonder what his father looked like? I guess it really doesn't matter, does it?"

"No mother, I don't think it does at this point. What matters now is that he is okay and so is his mama. Both need to meet and start this bonding process. Lord knows she's waited a lifetime for this...I wonder what she'll name him?"

"Knowing Terri, it will be a sophisticated name...like Taylor or Benjamin. Wouldn't surprise me if she didn't name him after a president or someone famous."

"Mother, does Gloria know what's happened?"

"As a matter of fact, I just got off the phone with her this morning, before we came to the hospital. She took the high school choral group up to Washington, DC to compete in the nationals. I told her what had happened and she asked if she needed to come home and be with the family. I assured her everybody was okay and there was no need for her to come home. She said she would come by and see Terri and the baby as soon as they got back. I just didn't want to worry her. Besides, she will see for herself when she gets back that everything is fine. Mother's just know these things."

Chapter 26

"Terri, can you hear me? Squeeze my hand as hard as you can if you can hear anything. We may have to give her a few more hours until the sedative wears off. People react differently to different drugs. It just may take her a little longer to come around. I'm not concerned yet. We'll give her another eight hours and if she still is not responding, then we'll try a different approach. In the meantime, this is what I want each of you to do while you are in her room. Talk to her as if she is sitting right here in front of you, alert and oriented. Do anything you can to include her in your conversations. This is a constant stimulus that she needs to recognize and feel comfortable with when she hears it. I'll come back later this afternoon to check on her. Let the nursing staff know ASAP if there are any changes. I feel confident she will come around. Her pupils are equal and reactive, her color is good, vitals signs are stable and there is no indication of infection. So, I believe she will make a full recovery."

~

"I think I like this color for the baby's room and this one for the rest of the upstairs. What do you think?"

"Well, Mr. Carter, we'll paint it whatever color you want...I just hope it's the one Terri wants. Hey, who's that driving up the driveway?"

"I'm not sure. I'm not even sure I've seen that truck before. Let's wait and see who gets out of the truck first before we go down there."

"Hello...anyone here?"

"Oh, that's Aubrey from the hospital. I hope there's nothing wrong!"

"Hi guys, how is everything going? Putting on the final touches, I see."

"Is Terri okay? I mean, has anything happened?"

"No no, everything is fine. Actually, there's been no change. I didn't mean to startle you. I just stopped by thinking you may need some help with color chips for the paint and carpeting. Have you made any decisions yet?"

"Aubrey, as a matter of fact we were just discussing the colors when you drove up. You couldn't have timed it any better! Okay, this is what we were looking at for the baby's room and then I picked this color for the rest of the upstairs. What do you think?"

"Let's see, Terri was really looking more at this color for the baby's room and this one for the rest of the upstairs."

"Aubrey, I actually like those better! I'm glad you knew which ones she wanted!"

"Me too...I'm glad I could help. Is there anything else I can do while I'm here?"

"I can't think of anything...the only thing we needed to complete were the color specs."

"Well, if you're sure...If you need any more information, don't hesitate to call. I'm going to stop by the hospital now to check on Terri and the baby. I'll call if there's any change, okay?"

"Okay, keep me posted. I'll stop by the hospital later too and check on them. I can't wait to hold my grandson!"

~

"Terri...Terri...can you hear me?"

Yes, I can hear you Aubrey. Why does she keep asking me that?

"I'm starting to get a little concerned about her recovery. I knew she would have a harder time recovering because of the trauma she endured in the car wreck. I just didn't think it would take her this long to come out of the drug-induced state."

"What do you think is happening Aubrey?"

"I'm not sure Jackie...I'm just not sure. I am going to contact her doctor and speak with him about it. Besides, he would want to know that she hasn't fully recovered. I'll be right back."

Aubrey left the room and I was left to ponder, once again, what was really happening to me. Maybe if I focused really hard, I could move my hand or something. I knew Jackie was still in the room. If I could get her attention in some way...to let her know I could hear her and Aubrey. Focus Terri, just focus.

"What did he say Aubrey?"

"I didn't get to talk to him, so I left a message on his voice mail. But, I want to try something he said before he left yesterday."

"Where are you going now?"

"To the nursery. I'll be right back."

Aubrey soon left again and I tried even harder to focus on moving something, hoping that Jackie or someone would notice.

"Terri? If you can hear me, I want you to focus on this description. I want you to try and feel what your son feels like on your skin. He is here now, asleep in my arms. His hand is closed, but I am moving it across the top of your hand. Can you feel it?"

Oh my God...I have waited for this moment for what seemed liked a lifetime and now, I can't even see him. His skin is so soft and his hand is so tiny. It feels like it's no bigger than a quarter.

"I want you to feel his cheek against yours and the faint smell of..."

"Aubrey, I thought I saw her hand move! Watch her hand..."

"Terri, your son is right here waiting for you to wake up. He's ready to go home now...with his mama. He wants to start his life with you. For that matter, I'm ready too. I am so ready to lie down beside you every night, wake up with you in the mornings, and live our lives together until..."

"Aubrey, there it goes again! Look!"

"Jackie, go get a nurse, quickly!"

Jackie left in a hurry to find a nurse at the nurse's station. She soon returned by throwing the door wide open and allowing the nurse to get ahead of her.

"What is it Dr. Shannon?"

"We thought we saw some movement in her hand, but we're not sure."

"Terri, the nurse is here now and we want you to show her how you can move your hand." I know you can do it, if you focus really hard!"

Aubrey, I would like nothing more than to wake up, see my son and go home so that we can start our family together. Damn it! Why can't I open my eyes?

The door was flung open again and in walked mom, with another nurse following quickly behind her.

"What's going on?"

212

"Mom, we think Terri is trying to wake up. I thought I saw her move her hand a minute ago. Ssh, Aubrey is talking to her now, trying to get her to open her eyes."

"Come on Terri, wake up and open your eyes. We're all here and pulling for you."

"What is happening now Aubrey?"

"I'm not sure, but I have a request..."

"Sure, name it!"

"Would all of you mind stepping outside for just a minute? I want to try something that might bring her out of this sleep."

"Okay, we're out of here."

I heard everyone leave, including the nurses, and just when I thought I would hear Aubrey's voice, I didn't. Instead, I heard the door close. For an instant, I believed I was all alone. How strange this felt. But then, I felt her hand take mine.

"Terri, I know you can hear me. I want to talk to you for a minute. The doctor told us that we should talk to you as if you were sitting right here in front of us, alert and oriented."

Yes Aubrey, I remember him saying that...

"Well, I guess now is a good time to tell you what I've wanted to for a long time. Since there is no one here in the room with us or to interrupt me, I can talk to you without worry. I don't want to lose my train of thought. So, here goes...I have thought and thought about how I would encourage you out of this drug-induced sleep. It finally dawned on me that I could encourage you with words from the heart."

Words from the heart? What could she possibly tell me that I don't already know?

"I never thought I would be saying this to you, because I lost you once, long ago. I never really expected to see you again, let alone be in a relationship with you. The first time I saw you at that party, I fell in-love with you. The second time I saw you was in my clinic. I fell in-love with you all over again. Yes, I am in-love with you and want to spend the rest of my life with you...and your son...I want us to be a family. I can't go home alone anymore. I just miss you so much when we're apart. Even Jasper misses you terribly! I want to go home with you Terri. I want to start living this dream that both of us have had for so long...the dream of having our own little family. Is that what you want?"

As I lay there, listening to her words of encouragement, I couldn't help but remember the night she took me home when it was snowing. The Red Tail Hawk finally decided to unveil her vulnerability. She decided to trust, just for a moment, show herself in plain sight and within touching distance. Something I had waited through each of the changing seasons to see. Why she waited until that night, I couldn't know for sure. But, I could speculate that it might have been her way of telling us that no matter how quickly or badly we wanted something to happen, patience was the answer. Aubrey had waited a long time to reconnect with me and I had prayed my heart would heal. What once seemed impossible was now inevitable. Timing was everything.

"You can come in now, but visiting hours are almost over for tonight."

"All right dear, we won't stay but just a few minutes. It's such a shame that she hasn't responded yet."

"I know, Mrs. Carter, but I don't think it will be much longer."

"We're going to go on and grab some supper. Would you like to join us, Aubrey?"

"Thanks, but I think I'll keep trying to get through to her for a little while longer."

"Okay dear, goodnight."

"I'll call you if there's any change. Good night."

~

"Dr. Shannon? Dr. Shannon, are you awake?"

"Yes, I'm awake. What is it?"

"Do you want to feed him before it gets too late?"

"Sure, I'll feed him."

"Any luck with Terri, yet?"

"No, not yet. But I think it will be soon."

"I know you must be tired. It's hard always running up to the hospital like this night after night. Why don't you just stay here tonight? We'll bring in a cot and you can just bunk here. What do you say about that?"

"Actually, I am tired. I think I'll take you up on your offer."

"Good, it's settled. I'll make the arrangements. Have you had dinner?

"No, but I'm not very hungry. Some hot tea might be nice."

"I can arrange that, too."

"Okay, I like this idea more and more. Thanks for the invite."

"You're welcome doctor."

V.A. Buck

Chapter 27

Do you remember how it felt to wake up from a nightmare where you were falling from an enormous height? If you've never experienced the feeling, let me be the first to tell you what a horrifying feeling it can be. It's like watching yourself in slow motion, dropping aimlessly faster and faster toward the ground. You can feel the dropping motion in your stomach, as if you have just gone over a dip in the road, but didn't expect it. You're watching yourself falling closer and closer to the ground, with reluctant anticipation from the impact of the hit that you will experience. The wind is so strong that you can barely breathe [like sticking your head out of a car window, when it's speeding seventy mile per hour]. You keep asking yourself over and over, will I survive this? You continue to fall for what feels like all night long. Then, you realize you're getting closer and closer to the ground. Cringing, once you see what's about to happen, you suddenly wake up, lying in a pool of sweat. Your mouth ajar, eyes fixed, staring in utter confusion. You're panting like you've been running a marathon. It's one of those things you can't prepare yourself for, yet you never forget the impact. That's how it felt to finally wake up.

I was jolted out of my sleep from a nightmare. I can't remember what I was dreaming, but I guess it doesn't matter. I had no idea how long I had been asleep, but from the looks of my room filled with flowers, balloons and cards, I would bet I had been here for awhile. I felt like a Mack Truck had run over me. Had I been dreaming about a car wreck or did it really happen? Gazing around the room, I spotted someone asleep on a cot. Whoever it was, I didn't want to wake them.

I saw my door beginning to open when in walked a nurse with the biggest smile on her face. I smiled back. I put my finger over my mouth as if to tell her to be quiet. The nurse looked over and whispered, "she would want to know you are awake."

"Who is it?"

"That's Dr. Shannon. She has been coming up here for several nights checking on you and your son to make sure that both of you are okay."

"What happened?"

"You don't remember?"

"I'm not sure...was I dreaming or was there really a car wreck?"

"No, you weren't dreaming, all of you were in a car wreck."

"Who is all of us?"

"You and your parents. They are sore and stiff, but fine."

"Is my son okay?"

"Yes, he's fine. He's in the nursery. While you were still asleep a few hours ago, Dr. Shannon fed him. So, he won't be ready for a few more hours, yet."

"Have you seen my sister?"

"I'm not sure if I have or not. Why do you ask?"

"She was suppose to be coming in soon, but I wasn't sure when."

"I've seen several people in your room, but I'm not sure who your sister is."

"Oh, okay. She's probably not here yet."

"How do you feel? Any soreness, stiffness, or pain?"

"Actually, I feel like I've been hit by a Mack Truck."

"You pretty much were...the impact was all on your side of the car. You actually took the brunt of the impact...and you were very lucky. My understanding about the whole thing was that you had just called your family to come get you because your water had broken and you were in labor. The wreck happened on the way to the hospital. Good thing you were just a few blocks away."

"I really don't remember much of anything about the wreck. What happened after they brought us to the hospital?"

"They had to do a cesarean delivery because of the trauma you suffered in the wreck. After the delivery, you started hemorrhaging. They had to take you back into surgery..."

"Back into surgery? For what?"

"Terri, they had to stop the massive hemorrhaging from the uterus. And, because you lost a lot of blood, you were given a blood transfusion. They finally decided to put you in a drug-induced sleep for awhile so that your body would have a chance to heal."

"How long have I been asleep?"

"You've been asleep for four days."

"Four days? It was that bad?"

"It was touch and go for awhile. But, it's all behind you and all you need to do now is gain your strength back so that you can go home and enjoy your son!"

"You're right about that and I can't wait to see him! By the way, what time is it?"

"It's six o'clock, why?"

"When's breakfast? I'm hungry."

The nurse left the room to get some food and while she was gone, I looked around at all of the arrangements of flowers scattered across the room and cards taped on the wall. It must have been an ordeal. Aubrey was still asleep on the cot. She looked so peaceful, but I wanted to wake her to let her know I was okay.

"Aubrey? Aubrey, are you awake?"

Aubrey began to stir in the covers, trying to wake up.

"Is it time to feed him again?"

"Aubrey?"

Slowly, she pulled off the covers, sat up on the cot, shook her head, trying to wake herself enough to feed the baby. Her eyes still closed, I watched her as she yawned furiously. She looked so tired. Suddenly, I saw her stand up quickly and turn toward me. She grabbed her robe and stumbled over to my bed. Her hair was all over her head, eyes swollen and barely open. But a huge smile was spread across her face.

"Terri, are you finally awake? My God, we have been waiting for four days for you to wake up! How do you feel?"

"I feel like I've been hit by a Mack Truck! At least that's what I've been telling everyone. I don't remember a whole lot...I thought maybe there had been a wreck, but I wasn't sure, because I thought I'd dreamed it. I guess not, huh?"

"No, you didn't dream it at all. The wreck was pretty massive. In fact, you and your son are very lucky to be alive. If you had been further away in the city somewhere, I don't think either of you would've had a very good prognosis. Anyway, now that you are finally awake, you will be able to see your son for the first time! How do you feel about that?"

Terri's face dropped as she tried to prop herself up on the pillow. Her emotions overcame her as she tried not to look at Aubrey. She sat with her hands in her lap and then she folded her arms across her chest. It was obvious she was uncomfortable about something. Aubrey sat down on the side of the bed, raised Terri's chin up with her hand until their eyes met. With a sigh, Terri finally conceded that she owed Aubrey an explanation.

"Aubrey, I'm actually really nervous about seeing him for the first time. I mean, I'm excited about seeing him and holding him, but I'm afraid I won't know what to do...I just haven't been around children like most people, you know?"

"You will be fine. Taking care of your child is an innate thing. Your motherly instincts will take over and in some strange way, you'll know exactly what to do. It's a woman thing, sensing exactly what your child needs. Besides, I'll be there to help, remember?"

"I remember... and I am so ready to go home Aubrey. I know you are going to think I am crazy when I tell you this, but I think you are just as ready to go home, aren't you?

"What do you mean?"

"I don't know how to explain this, but there were so many things I heard you say while I was here in the hospital. I only hope I can remember them all."

"Why would I think you're crazy? And what do you mean things you heard...you mean, things you dreamed about?"

"No, things that were said while I was asleep. I heard everything...but I couldn't respond. Trying to remember it all, is the problem."

"What things? Can you give me an example of something you thought you heard? Was it something I said or someone else?"

"Well, the best that I can recall, it was you, Jackie and my parents mostly. But I'm not sure...sometimes, I

221

believed I was dreaming, because I didn't think Jackie was in town yet. Is she in?"

"As a matter of fact, she is. She came in when the wreck happened. Now, tell me what you can remember."

"Okay, the first thing I remember was you coming into the room and telling my dad and I think Jackie what kind of shape I was in. That I was critical, and would be for at least the next forty-eight hours. That must have been after the wreck happened."

"That's amazing...you were completely out of it when we you brought you up to your room."

"What I remember the most was how scared you were when you laid your head on my shoulder. You finally fell asleep. When your hand touched mine, I could feel you trembling. I knew you were so scared."

"You knew all that was happening?"

"Yes Aubrey, but there's more. I remember you telling me how you were ready to go home and start our family together. That you were in-love with me and how you hated going home alone. Even Jasper missed me."

"Did I say that about Jasper?"

"Yes, you did...and not only did you talk about Jasper, but you even gave me a play-by-play action when you fed my son for the first time. You said how much he looked like his mama and hoped he didn't mind you calling him 'little one'. I thought that was so sweet."

"I can't believe you heard all that...I guess the medical field will want to interview you for more information! You might be the next medical marvel! By the way, have you picked out a name for your son yet?"

"Oh my Lord, no, I haven't. I haven't even seen him yet! I've had a few in mind...want to hear my choices?"

"Of course...what are they?"

"Okay, they are in no certain order. What about Joseph Robert, Alexander Lee, Nicholas Edward or William

Henry Carter. What do you think about the first and middle names?"

"Well, your mother was right about one thing?"

"What's that?"

"She said you would probably give him a sophisticated name. Any of those names would be perfect. Have you narrowed them down any?"

"No, that's the problem. I like them all because they have at least one of the family's name in either the first or the middle name. I guess I'll know when I see my son...what name will fit him the best."

"Well, get ready because here he is..."

I watched as the nurse brought him in the room all wrapped up in a blanket with a toboggan on this head. When she finally laid him in my arms, it was an instant bond. His eyes opened and looked into mine for the first time. I just stared at him in awe of how beautiful he was. His face was perfectly round, with a tiny little nose and precious ears. He was perfect, with ten little fingers and ten little toes. He had no hair, but peach fuzz, as we call it in the south.

"How much did he weigh when he was born?"

"I believe he weighed eight pounds, two ounces and he was nineteen inches long. A good size baby!"

"And he is okay? He doesn't have any abnormalities?"

"No, everything is fine. All the reports on him were perfect."

I looked at Aubrey for a moment and I could tell she was getting emotional. She just looked at me, bit her lip slightly, and smiled that wonderful smile. She took a deep breath and sighed while shaking her head. You could tell that her thoughts were good, whatever they were.

"Aubrey, which name do you think best suits him?"

"My goodness, I think he looks like a 'Nicholas Edward'...what do you think?"

I looked down at this bundled baby who had soft skin, beautiful eyes, long arms and legs. The tiniest features were his fingers, toes, and ears. Somehow, I knew he would grow up to be strong, special, and everything a mother dreamed he would become.

"I'm not sure...maybe that one or William Henry."

"I like that one, too. But, you have plenty of time to decide on a name."

"I know, but it's already been four days... He's going to think his mama doesn't want him if I don't give him a name soon!"

"Look who's here..."

The door to her room suddenly opened and Jackie entered with mother and dad right behind her.

"Jackie! You did come!"

"Of course I did squister! How are you feeling, now that you have been asleep for four days?"

"Sore, stiff...but I am glad to be awake now so that I can finally see my son. Isn't he beautiful?"

"Yes he is...we have been admiring him for the past few days. Speaking of which, have you decided on a name yet?"

"We were just discussing that. Actually, I think I have.

Everybody, meet Nicholas Edward Carter."

Epilogue

After a few more days in the hospital, the day finally came to take Nicholas home. I was very appreciative both Aubrey and my family were coming over to help me, because I wasn't allowed to lift anything over ten pounds. And, I surely didn't want to pop a stitch.

Nicholas' room had been finished with a beautiful bedroom suite, fit for a boy. Aubrey and Dad made sure the colors were perfect for the entire upstairs, including the baby's room. Even though I slept most of the time while I was in the hospital, I was still tired. I guess my body just needed to take the time to heal.

Mom and Jackie were constantly in and out of the house helping take care of Nicholas and myself. Mom was busy cooking her famous recipes and Dad was coming over to make sure all the renovation issues had been finalized. Jackie was my chauffeur, taking me everywhere I needed to go. She soon announced she wasn't going back to Texas and that she planned on relocating back home. We were all very ecstatic about the whole idea. I missed her being around and doing things together, but I understood she needed her own space to live her life. And too, she has wanted a little one of her own for quite some time now. Somehow, I knew she had gained her independence from us. Gloria came over for a brief stay, visiting with Nicholas and talking with dad.

Not long after I arrived home from the hospital, Aubrey sold her house and moved in with Nicholas and I. Jasper moved in too. He loved chasing butterflies and hummingbirds, which were much too quick for him to catch. He continued to adjust to the country living atmosphere by watching all the different aquatic birds from the shoreline, including the great blue heron. Aubrey was getting adjusted, too and seemed very happy living with us. I couldn't believe she was willing to give up her gorgeous home for a cabin in the woods. I told her that if this home ever became too small, we could always add another floor on top. Aubrey had ideas of her own when she surprised me with new pool plans to erect on the property. Everybody loved the idea, especially since it would give family time with Nicholas. Besides, I'm sure dad wouldn't pass up the opportunity to do some landscaping work out here. He loved it out here as much as we did. Especially me, since I pretty much grew up out here. It's important to me that my son appreciates the wilderness and respect the wildlife, instead of hunting it for game.

The Red Tail Hawk has continued her refuge here and so have her young. They have made themselves more visible and continue to fly closer to us. The Blue Jays have become territorial and are fighting the hawks for air space. But, the hawks have become more protective since their young have been born. I know how that feels to protect your young. I've waited a lifetime for what I have now and I won't let anything destroy it. How ironic she has become in my life...another moralizing story.

Since I have moved here, the Red Tail Hawk has been in my life and she has shown me many things. She taught me lessons of insight, truth, and openness. Aubrey and I are closer than we have ever been. She loved seeing Nicholas in my arms. She would join me in the kitchen and watch as I fed him a bottle. She was right about the motherly instincts taking over, too. It just seemed so simple, I guess. I really had nothing to be afraid of anymore. Seeing Nicholas and Aubrey every day, I can't imagine what my life would be like without them. In fact, I can't imagine my life any other way. I am finally complete.

V.A. Buck

About the Author

After completing her Master's degree from the University of Toledo, the author relocated near the Great Smoky Mountains of Tennessee, where her fictitious novels originate.

She's admitted she'd always wanted to write since her Creative Writing class days in high school. The author further explained that she'd always had an active imagination. She often tells her friends and family that having the desire to write, combined with her active imagination are gifts. She confesses that despite her chosen career, writing is her passion.

She has also written a series of children's books, 'Sabrina's Adventures', which are based upon her tabby cat's curious explorations. Stay tuned for her next bold mission. She will steal your heart.